Dear Mom and Dad

Dear Mom and Dad

A Love Letter to Our Parents

by Amy Siebert & Kim Stille

Dear Mom and Dad

A Love Letter To Our Parents

© 2020 by Amy Siebert & Kim Stille

Windy City Publishers
2118 Plum Grove Road, #349
Rolling Meadows, IL 60008

www.windycitypublishers.com

Published in the United States of America

ISBN#:
978-1-953294-01-2

Library of Congress Control Number:
2020914426

WINDY CITY PUBLISHERS
CHICAGO

To all the people who are broken and wounded,
who have felt pain and known heartache.
Everyone suffers, everyone has a story,
but this story is ours...

Contents

Foreword

By Mary Fox Clausen

$\mathcal{I}$ve known Amy and Kim for over half of my life. Amy and I went to the same high school growing up, but we didn't get to know each other until we became roommates during our college years. I thank God for that time. To put it simply, Amy was a dream. Sincerely, she was everything you could ask for in a roommate—sweet, honest, kind, funny (oh, the stories), considerate, spiritual, and a true confidante. We had a ball during those two years we shared an apartment together, but we always made sure we never got too carried away. I guess you could say that Amy and I are the kind of people who like to stay inside the lines when we color. We like to have a good time, but we tend to follow the rules.

Our relationship came so easily, and in no time, we became fast friends. I had a good feeling early on that we would stay close long after school was over (that seemed even more probable after I set her up on a blind date her sophomore year with the man that would eventually become her husband). It's amazing when I think about it, but Amy and I have never had a disagreement. Not one harsh word between us in over twenty-five years. There's never been a reason. She truly is one of the most genuine and caring souls I've ever met. She was my rock back in college, and she still is today. Whenever I need good, solid counsel or a tender, loving ear, Amy is almost always the first person I go to. As we like to say, God sure knew what he was doing when he made us roommates.

I got to know Kim when I spent time with Amy and her family. As the years went by, Kim grew from being "Amy's little sister" to my friend. It's been an absolute joy watching Kim grow and flourish in life—as a teacher, as a wife, as a mother, and as a person. Kim shares so many of those same incredible qualities that I used to describe her sister, but where Amy walks into a room and can light it up, Kim downright takes center stage. Often the life of the party, you can't help but be drawn to her infectious laughter and her larger than life personality. Kim's not afraid to color outside of the lines, and that's something I admire so much about her.

It was easy to see why these two sisters were so likable and fun to be around. They came from an incredible family anchored by a loving and nurturing mother and an adoring and fun-loving father. Their family bond was truly enviable. To me, they acted how parents and children should act towards one another—with love and respect and lots of laughter. But like all families, they weren't immune to tough times, and some of those times would instantly change their lives forever. Some say a person's true colors come out in the face of adversity. Well, if that's true, I think this family is a shining example of how to handle those tough times. As I've walked beside Amy during some of these ebbs and flows, it's been inspirational to see how she and Kim have leaned on each other as they've tackled some of their family's toughest trials. It's like watching a symphony at times. Without missing a beat, they instantly come together, pray, formulate a plan and get to work. Most impressively, they seem to do it all so effortlessly and with love, and hope, and in true family-style, with lots of laughter.

Many of us who are close to Amy have encouraged her throughout the years to write a book. She has a natural gift to bring stories to life through her writing and has modestly blogged for years about everyday life with her two hilarious boys and her amazing husband (who himself has a testimony that is bookworthy). During a particularly trying season that the family was going through, one where Amy and Kim found themselves in the trenches again and again, Amy shared with me that she was finally ready to put her stories into print. I think the overwhelming emotional roller coaster she had been riding pushed her to a point where she had nowhere else to go with everything she was feeling and had to get it out. She said she wanted it to be a love letter to her parents, and I thought there couldn't have been a more perfect story for Amy to write at that moment. When she told me that she and Kim were going to write the book together, I was beyond thrilled. As it turns out, Kim has an incredible gift for storytelling as well. Little did I know how captivating their tales would become when told by each sister through their own unique lens. I shouldn't have been surprised. Once again, it's like watching a symphony…

What you're holding in your hands now is the culmination of this labor of love. A love letter that honestly, hilariously, and sometimes heartbreakingly, recounts some of the most important and pivotal moments shared between two sisters and their parents. I hope you enjoy this wonderful ride down memory lane they're about to take you on. Without even realizing it, I found myself remembering some of my own family memories, both good and bad, with a little more gratitude and a lot more grace. I hope this memoir does the same for you.

Chapter 1

Our Childhood (the '80s)

...and how from infancy you have known the Holy Scriptures,
which are able to make you wise for salvation through faith in Christ Jesus.

~2 Timothy 3:15

Amy

Dad was the family comedian and everyone found him hysterical. His humor was one of the things my mom loved so dearly about him. He had this gift of making the funniest faces, and within seconds you'd crack up. His faces were classic and his sense of humor was limitless. As a child, I watched countless hours of Chicago Cubs baseball with him, and many of our family vacations, centered around, visits to Wrigley Field.

Mom was a teacher and didn't work during the summer. She dropped us off at activities, took us to the pool, and hosted friends at the house. One of the things Dad loved during the summertime was eating lunch with his family. We would sit down at the dining room table together and enjoy the sandwiches Mom had prepared. Dad's favorite was Mom's homemade ham salad with Thousand Island dressing. Dad's mood was always great during those "eat from home" summer lunches. He would joke around with Kim and me, tease my mom, and turn on his favorite soap opera, *All My Children*. For sixty minutes each day we were mesmerized by Erica Kane and her antics, and before we knew it, Dad needed to jump back in the car for the ten-minute drive back to work. This was the '80s—a great decade for my family, especially my Dad. Dad was a master carpenter. When he and Mom got married, they bought an older, somewhat run-down home that required a lot of work. My paternal grandfather was a builder, and for years Dad worked for Grandpa, learning the skills of the trade. All of those skills paid off. Through the years we watched our home transform into a beautiful masterpiece where family and friends gathered. Dad gutted and rebuilt the kitchen, tore out the dining room wall, installed a sliding glass door, made custom cabinetry for our dining room, built a deck, remodeled the basement, and added a bathroom. One summer he and a neighbor put a new roof on our house. What a mess that was, but Dad got the job done. Obviously, Dad had boundless patience when it came to remodeling projects. After saving for years, they put in new carpet. I picked an ice blue carpet for my bedroom, on which I promptly spilled purple nail polish! I remember Mom and I frantically trying to get the polish out, all the while Mom saying, "We have to get this out before your dad gets home." From behind us, Dad's voice calmly rang out, "Too late." Amazingly, he took the carpet disaster in stride.

Nobody could vacation like Dad—except maybe my sister. He loved trips and took great pride in planning them (something as an adult I find stressful and exhausting). When I was thirteen and Kim was nine, our parents took us to Disney World. My parents saved for years for this trip. Of course, Dad savored planning each detail of the entire trip. He took two weeks off work, and we piled into our Chevy Celebrity. Kim had her pillows, blankets, and stuffed animals (some things never change), and I had my Walkman—after all, it was the '80s. We started our trip with a stop in Savannah, Georgia, then headed to the great state of Florida. We went to Disney World for six days and enjoyed other stops on the way home including Myrtle Beach. We finished the last leg of the trip in North Carolina, visiting Dad's older sister Susan. Dad loved every second of that trip.

I was a strong-willed child. Mom often laughs because when she was pregnant with me, she prayed for a "challenging" child. God delivered! I tested her at every turn. Mom lined her bookshelves with child-rearing books. Her favorite was *The Strong-Willed Child* by Dr. James Dobson. I never liked to venture much outside my comfort zone. Mom pushed, or rather demanded, that I pursue extracurricular activities in which I had no interest. In middle school I played clarinet in the school band. By the time I began my freshman year of high school, I hated playing the clarinet, and honestly, I stunk at it. I begged Mom to let me quit, but she was having none of it. She forced me to be a part of the high school band, which in turn meant participating in band camp. I remember marching around in the late August heat, playing an instrument I despised, and cursing Mom under my breath the entire time. Mom was tough, but she was also reasonable. Although she forced me to play my freshman year, she promised that if things didn't turn around for me, and if I still felt the same about band at the end of the year, I could quit. Somehow, I made it through, despite holding last chair (the lowest-ranked player) and honking that stinking clarinet my entire freshman year. As soon as the school year ended, I quit with absolutely no regrets.

Additionally, during my middle school years, Mom forced me to go to church camp. Furious, I wondered, didn't she know I had better things to do with my time during the summer? I also knew that arguing with Mom got me nowhere. I had to at least try *something* to satisfy her. Unlike band, I went to church camp and I loved it. At first, I didn't want to go, but as the week went on, I loved it more and more. I went back to church camp every year after that, eventually becoming a camp counselor. My love of church camp spilled into youth mission trips in high school, which I adored just as much as church camp. Church camp and mission trips provided me with a firm foundation for my faith. Spiritual seeds were planted during those trips, and I am forever grateful to Mom for her diligence.

Yes, the '80s were good. I have wonderful memories of when we rented a VHS player and watched *Ghostbusters* while roasting marshmallows in our fireplace. We had neighborhood block parties where the parents would sit along the street and chat while all of the kids ran around shooting each other with water guns.

I was a little girl who loved her daddy so much. I wanted to be just like him. One time when I was five, I went as far as taking my shirt off to run with him around the neighborhood because he had his shirt off. I was Daddy's little girl. When I held his hand, I could only grab onto his pinky because his hand was so big and my fingers were so small. Some of our best conversations happened at bedtime when he did voiceovers for my teddy bear. I giggled as my big, fluffy, brown Molly Bear addressed hilarious comments in a variety of silly voices to "Mr. B." I never went a single night without my bear. In fact, that "Damn bear," as my sister liked to call her, went with us on every family vacation. Full disclosure, I still sleep with that "Damn bear," I just don't take her on vacation anymore—mostly because Amy says I'm being ridiculous.

Dad didn't just make us laugh, he sang to us as well. His favorite song was "Kumbaya My Lord." He would sing, "Someone's sleeping, Lord," and then he would make snoring noises, cracking me up. I thought he was the funniest guy ever. He tucked me in and kissed me goodnight. I laid in my beautiful oak sleigh bed—an heirloom from Dad's grandmother—drifting off to sleep. I remember tracing the marks in the wood with my finger. One of the shapes in the wood reminded me of a table with stools. It also had wooden slats on the sides holding it together. Those slats were about eight inches tall and made of very hard, tough wood. I know this because one time, Amy threw me down and whipped my head right into it. My ear bled a little; it really hurt, and I was crying and screaming, "I'm telling Mom." Amy was holding me down pleading with me not to tell her. Amy and I are super close—soul mates you might call us—but there was a time when she was not very nice to me! Like the time she put glue in my milk and I puked for days. Well, maybe not days, but I did get sick, and it was not nice of her to do that.

Dad loved Halloween. I remember one year he dressed as a woman. He had way too much fun with that costume. The best Halloween was when he plotted his outfit for weeks and wouldn't give any of us the slighted clue about it. We were all giddy with anticipation to see what silly costume he'd dreamed up. Well, we couldn't even imagine this get up: a giant green bug! He sported yellow tights, a giant blow-up head tied around his chin, his face painted green, and bug legs sprang from the sides of his bright yellow turtleneck. When he came around the corner to show off his well thought out, hilarious costume, we all roared with laughter. I was probably around ten or so at this time, so when we showed up over at my good friend Lindsay's house to go trick-or-treating, I wasn't so sure about Dad's costume. We found it super funny at home, but in public, around my friends, it might embarrass me. Fortunately, Lindsay and her family burst out laughing in appreciation of his craftwork. That unforgettable year, we cruised the neighborhood with our trick-or-treat bags in hand and a giant green bug trailing behind us!

Dad also loved other holidays, like Christmas. Every wintery Christmas morning he instructed Amy and me to sit at the top of the stairs, not allowing us to venture down until he checked to see if Santa came. He took his time and teased us. We waited anxiously, smiling and shivering with delight until Dad shouted, "Okay, he came. You can come down." We took off running down the steps like a herd of elephants to find all of our treasures under the tree, while Dad watched with joy in his eyes. He loved to see his family so happy.

Mom was tough, but nurturing. She chose sacrifice over selfishness. My fondest memories include helping her with dishes or running errands, because then we could talk and bond. She always listened and knew just what to say. She always took the time to set a good example and teach us to be good Christians. At Christmas time we always made sure to perform an act of kindness to help our community. Every year we undertook a different project. One year, Mom tasked us with discovering our own good deed to do for someone else. When I was probably seven or eight years old, I decided I would write a note to a neighbor who lived several blocks away. I had always admired the giant Christmas wreath adorning their chimney. I delivered the note with such pride. The elderly lady who answered the door looked touched by the nice gesture, making me realize why these random acts of kindness are important. Mom also made sure that the elderly neighbor across the street always had a hot meal (usually ham balls and scalloped corn) to enjoy on Christmas Eve. Mom stayed at home until I went into first grade. Being the younger sibling is sometimes hard, especially when you have a sister like Amy, who monopolized every second of our mother's time! When Amy went off to school and Dad went off to work, I felt thrilled to finally have Mom all to myself. I vividly remember when it was time to go to half-day Kindergarten, Mom would walk me to school every day holding my hand. I loved school, but boy I loved my mom more.

Mom always liked to call me her "life is a bowl full of cherries" baby because I was such an easy-going "life is good" kinda kid. My memories of my mom go far deeper than being my Girl Scout troop leader or making sure my homework was done. She instilled in us good values, always put my sister and me first, and loved us unconditionally.

Amy,

Although the '80s overall was a good decade for our family, there was one particular dark cloud. In 1983, Dad had his first affair. I was in the fourth grade and Kim was entering Kindergarten. I know this now as an adult, but as a nine-year-old, I remained clueless. He traveled a lot and met a woman in Atlanta, Georgia. One thing led to another, as all affairs do, and eventually Mom found out.

One fall afternoon right after school, my parents sat us down and told us Dad was temporarily moving out. I remember crying a lot and not having a good understanding of why my dad was leaving the household. My maternal grandparents came down that evening in an effort to bring some peace and calm. That night I couldn't fall asleep. My grandmother comforted me in our living room with a warm glass of milk. It's the only time in my life I can remember drinking warm milk.

An old friend of Dad's let him "borrow" his house, as the man traveled regularly for work. It was a small green ranch house across town. Kim and I spent time with Dad there. Even though it was such a difficult situation, I have fond memories of my time spent with Dad at that home. He seemed genuinely sad to be living without us. We never talked about when he would come back home or why he wasn't living with us in the first place. We just knew something had gone terribly wrong.

Fall turned into winter, and Christmas came and went without Dad. Christmas in our house was a big deal. Christmas Eve was always spent just the four of us, but that particular year we slept overnight at my grandparents. Before we left, Dad presented Kim and me with a dollhouse he made himself. We loved the gesture and played with it for years.

At our grandparents' house, Mom, Kim, and I went through the motions, but it didn't feel the same without Dad. After Christmas, we made the two-hour drive back home. When we had nearly reached our house, Mom said, "Girls, I have a surprise for you when you get home." Naturally, we bugged her to tell us what it was. When we pulled up in the drive, there was Dad's car. Dad was waiting for us in the house, and he was back for good! We were elated.

At the time Mom and Dad never told us why he moved out, which seems wise. As kids, we would not have been able to process the adult issues our parents had. Quite frankly, I don't think I would have cared. All I cared about was that my dad was back home and life as we knew it could finally get back to normal. It wasn't until years later that I learned the real reason Dad had moved out.

Kim

I was only five-years-old when Dad had his first affair. I actually have scant memory of this time. I do remember Dad's borrowed house—the small, one-bedroom ranch. I recall the open kitchen plan, and I remember him fixing us eggs for breakfast. As Amy and I grew into young adults, Mom could share a little more about this time in our lives. She told us that Dad had traveled to Atlanta, Georgia, for business, where he met the other woman. She explained that one time he had planned a hunting trip, which really just served as an excuse. He met the woman half way for a weekend rendezvous. Mom took us to our grandparents that weekend. Mom told her parents that Dad was on a hunting trip—surprising because he didn't hunt! This seemed fishy to our grandparents, setting off alarm bells. My dad eventually confessed to the affair; the guilt ate him alive! Fortunately, Amy and I remained completely oblivious to all of this. Wisely, our parents kept these details from us until we were adults. After the separation, things immediately returned to normal. We lived like a happy family again, enjoying family dinners, vacations, and holidays. Dad and Mom attended counseling with our minister, and life remained good for several years.

Amy

After Dad's first affair, he returned home, and as Kim said, things got back to a happy normal pretty quickly. For many years after the separation, we were able to create family memories that were long lasting. During my middle school years, Dad was there when I went to dances and played in band concerts. When I entered high school, he taught me how to drive. One summer while I was in high school, he took us to a Cubs game in Chicago, one of his favorite things to do. Another time, when I was sixteen and Kim twelve, we flew to Sanibel Island for a beach vacation. As usual, Dad planned the entire trip, and we had a ball. We even enjoyed a fancy dinner at The Bubble Room, and Kim and I wore matching flamingo outfits. As a family we talked about going to Hawaii for our next trip. At the time, I had no idea Sanibel Island would be our last family vacation. Hawaii was not to be.

Chapter 2

The Divorce

(August 1991 ~ May 1992)

Every child of divorce must walk a path of healing.
It will look different for every son and daughter but no one can deny
that the emotional relational bleeding needs attention long after papers are filed.

~Paul Maxwell

Amy

I struggled to put on my white, off the shoulder dress, not because it didn't fit, but because it was such a cute dress, and it didn't fit the occasion. It was a dress I felt good in. A dress I enjoyed wearing. It was August 1991. I was seventeen-years-old, getting ready to enter my senior year of high school. I had my future right in front of me. Although I didn't see it, and certainly wouldn't have been able to acknowledge it, I was smart, attractive, and funny. I made friends easily, and I was excited about my future. The possibilities were endless, but my primary focus was my parents' dissolving marriage. I enjoyed my senior year, but I faced a lot of tension watching their marriage dissolve into shambles. Mom and Dad may have tried, but they couldn't cover up their late-night arguments. Their marriage had quickly nosedived. Just two months earlier, Dad had taken Mom into Chicago for a weekend getaway to celebrate their upcoming twenty-year anniversary. It was just the two of them. They ate at fabulous restaurants and took carriage rides. He presented her with a beautiful diamond ring to mark the special occasion. Sadly, two months later, they found themselves at the beginning of the end of their relationship. I believe Dad was fully involved in his second affair at that time, but was doing a better job hiding it. I don't think Dad ever thought Mom would find out about this affair, and he believed that even if she did, she wouldn't leave him—after all, she'd forgiven him the last time. One particular August night, our family went out to celebrate my parents 20 year anniversary. What a joke! I knew Dad was having an affair, and Mom finally had enough with his drinking and womanizing. Still, we went out to eat as a family. It was the most uncomfortable dinner I can remember. We somehow made small talk and I excused myself several times to go to the bathroom.

Despite the tragic situation something positive and powerful grew from it: the strong bond between my sister and me. I was so thankful she was there experiencing the same pain I was. She was thirteen, and although younger siblings tend to annoy their older siblings I felt grateful we could share this mess together. By October, my dad had moved out, and by the time I graduated high school, they were divorced. Growing up down the street from each other, dating each other for years, attending church together regularly, had disappointingly not been enough to protect my parents' marriage from demise, and they became another statistic. Despite counseling, and lots of tears, my parents just couldn't make it work. With Mom now forty-one and Dad forty-three, they had spent more than half their lives knowing and loving each other. They would enter the second half of their lives without each other. They picked themselves up, dusted themselves off, and started brand-new chapters in their lives. *Alone.* I don't think either of them wanted to live without the other, but ultimately, my dad couldn't or wouldn't be faithful, and he choose a path that we didn't want for him. I'm certain it was not the path God wanted for any of us.

Kim

I was an awkward thirteen-year-old girl who knew exactly what was happening to my family. Retelling this part of our story is hard. It opens old wounds. Feelings of sadness and anger rush back like it happened yesterday. Although I don't remember that awful dinner, I do remember another significant night around that time. My good friend Lindsay's parents, Donna and Gary, were celebrating their twentieth, too, and we wanted to make dinner for our parents. We set the table, poured the wine, and slaved away in the kitchen. We were so excited about presenting the meal to our wonderful parents. I don't remember exactly what was on the menu, except for twice baked potatoes! I made Lindsay do most of the work. That's probably why they turned out so good. What wasn't so good was the sick feeling I had. It was supposed to be a happy occasion, but I remember feeling sad.

Amy alluded to my dad's womanizing. Sadly, I was a witness to his indiscretion. One night, I had a friend sleeping over. I knew something was going on when my mom abruptly left the house saying she would be back soon. My friend and I continued to listen to music while doing each other's hair. Soon, I heard my dad storm into the house. I turned up the music, told my friend I was going to get something, and headed downstairs to see what was going on. Hidden at the bottom of the steps, I heard yelling. I remember Mom shouting, "I saw you, BRAD! You, were cuddled up in that booth with so and so!" She used the woman's name, but I refuse to put it in this book. After hearing way more than any young girl should have to, I went back to my room to try to carry on with my slumber party.

A bit later in the evening, when Amy got back from being out with friends, I dove into her arms crying. While I reported everything I had heard, she held me, calmed me down, and made me feel better—as she always has. Man, I love my sister!

Still, my dad continued to date this woman, which was another one of his bad decisions. This affair obviously led to the divorce. Mom probably would have stayed if Dad was willing to change his behavior and seek counseling, but Dad had significant demons to fight at that time. He had a lot of internal struggles that I don't think any of us knew about, and we still don't. None of us knew how to help him. He chose alcohol and women to numb whatever he was feeling. If Dad were sitting here right now, he would say the best thing he ever did was marry my mom, and that he loved us girls with all his heart. He loved my mom and he loved being a family man, but like I said there was something inside him that wouldn't let him just be content. Mom once said to me, "Your dad was like a boulder rolling down a hill. If I didn't get myself and you girls out of the way, he would have taken us all down with him"

Amy,

Kim and I often laugh because each of us have different memories. Sometimes she will tell a story from our childhood, and I will look at her like she has two heads, having no clue what she is talking about. Kim met me by the back door when I came home that night and she did fall into my arms with a lot of tears. More than anything I wanted my dad out of the house. He was wreaking havoc on a home that was once stable and happy. As August ended and we entered September, I remember my mom sitting down in the living room with just me. She was crying and telling me she felt so terrible this was happening because it was my senior year of high school. I reminded Mom she had no choice; she had to ask Dad to leave. As a young and impressionable seventeen-year-old girl my mom demonstrated to me that although her entire world was crashing down around her, she loved herself and her girls enough to get out.

When Dad moved out in October 1991, he moved into a small apartment about ten minutes from our house. I don't remember visiting there much because, quite honestly, it was sad. When Dad moved out, he was angry, and that anger spilled into his relationship with Kim and me. I think he was shocked that my mom had finally had enough. Dad convinced himself and others that Mom left him because he was working too much. His womanizing and drinking were silent factors that he never mentioned. I was older this time around and could see what was really going on. I was upset that Dad continued to see this other woman. I was angry that he was angry, but most of all, I was disappointed in his decisions. Faith is what sustained Kim, my mom, and me. We knew that no amount of tears we cried compared to the tears God was crying over our broken family.

Kim,

Being a child of divorce and having a broken relationship with my father has had an impact on my life as an adult. I was constantly searching for male approval and spending time with all the wrong kinds of guys. Until I met my husband. I did not make it easy for him to stick around. I pushed him away because I thought I was undeserving of a healthy relationship where a man could be trusted. We have been happily married for fifteen years. We share similar values, respect and love each other, and have fun together. We have a twelve-year-old girl and a nine-year-old boy. Being a wife and mother has helped me to wrap my head around what happened to me as a child. As I watch my daughter grow and change, it brings me right back to when I was that age. She reminds me so much of myself. She is strong-willed, but sweet. She is happy go lucky and inquisitive. She understands things, but is still so naive. I watch her hold her dad's hand, talk to him, and cuddle with him. They have such a special bond. My dad and I did, too. That was until I turned around age thirteen, when things started to change. My dad wasn't around much at bedtime anymore to sing to me or make me laugh. Often, there were three of us around the dinner table instead of four.

I remember one night when Dad told me he was going for a run. I watched him take off down the street through my bedroom window. Several hours went by. It was getting dark. Why wasn't Dad back from his run? I sat on the floor by that window gazing out into the dark street. I sat there for a long time with tears in my eyes worrying about him and wondering where he was. I later found out he was at a bar. That is where he was starting to spend all his time. It got to the point that he was never home, and when he was, we didn't laugh or have fun anymore. Mom and Dad were fighting a lot, and on that October day when they sat us down to tell us Dad was leaving, I not only saw it coming, I was glad. I wanted him out. Mom, Amy, and I have talked a lot about this time in our life since we have become adults. I am so glad my mom had the courage to walk away. She saved herself, my sister, and especially me. There are a lot of things I am grateful to my mom for and this was one of many. I know it broke her heart. It broke all of our hearts, but it was the right thing to do.

I spent many years being very angry at my dad. Angry at him for what he did to my mom. Angry at him for not being the father he should have been to me. And angry about the choices he made.

When the divorce papers came in, and my parents had to separate their things, my mom noticed my dad wanted to take the antique bed and shelves from my room. Yes, they did belong to his grandmother, but those pieces had been a part of my bedroom since I was a small child, and all of my special knick-knacks and books filled those shelves. Mom called to plead with him not to take this furniture. We thought he had agreed to let me keep them until I was eighteen.

The day my dad arrived to move his things out of the house, my mom asked her father to be there since Mom, Amy, and I would not be. We returned and the house seemed somewhat empty. I ran up to my room. My bed was there, but in the corner there was nothing but empty space. All my books and knick-knacks were shoved off to the side. Dad had taken the shelves! I burst into tears.

Amy and I immediately got in the car and drove over to Dad's. She was going to get my shelves back for me. How could Dad do this to her little sister? When we got to his apartment complex we couldn't figure out which building he lived in. Apparently, God *didn't* want Amy to do this for me. When we got back home, Mom had to do it. She looked up Dad's address. When we got there, we marched in like we were on a mission. Mom thrust open the door, said a few things, and then just picked up some shelf pieces. I just stood there sobbing, grabbing pieces of my shelves off the floor as we left.

Amy

In May 1992, I graduated from high school and left for college in August. It was the first time in my life I was fully aware of the special people God places in your life at just the right time. He has continued to do this in my life, but Mary was my first (of many) blessings. I was raw when I left for college. I was angry, sad, and had no idea who I was. Mary was everything I wasn't. She was mature, strong in her faith, and the kindest person I'd ever been around. She spoke the truth to me when I desperately needed to hear it. She introduced me to my husband and continues to this day to be one of my most trusted spiritual confidants and dearest friends. She was also all too familiar with the pain of divorce. Her parents had split years earlier, after a battle even uglier and more hurtful than my parents' had been. Still, she harbored no bitterness, no anger. She worked her butt off for everything she got. I had accepted Christ when I was eleven, but I didn't know what it meant to be a follower of Christ. Mary trusted Him for all things. I wish that during my college years I would have trusted God. I wish I could have left all my burdens at the cross, but I didn't. I wish I could have prayed my way through all my worries, but I didn't. I thought I had it all under control.

Mary helped me navigate the waters with my dad. Dad was unpredictable during my college years. I didn't see him much, and it was evident that back at home he had no interest in seeing Kim either, even though she lived just across town. My parents paid my college expenses, and I was able to graduate (yes, I was on the five-year plan) later without debt. I was and am incredibly grateful for such a gift. Thankfully, Dad did his part to provide for my education. This gift was not without some strings attached. Although he agreed to pay my utilities each month, before he would write me a check I had to make photocopies of my bills and mail them to him. Once he had reviewed the bills to ensure the amount was what I had told him, he would write me a check. It was a process I grew to hate. It stung every month when the message, loud and clear, was that he didn't trust me.

Kim

I too had a Mary come into my life during this time. Her name was Amy, which I know is really confusing because my sister's name is Amy, so let's just call her Beth. I was angry, sad, and had no idea who I was. I walked into my middle school classroom and knew no one. I was awkward, lonely, and scared. Beth had long beautiful hair and a very friendly disposition. She is still the nicest person I know. She also understood the pain of divorce. Her parents had split years earlier. It was just she and her mom. Her dad didn't see her much either. We had a lot in common, and we quickly became inseparable friends. I invited her to join my family's church, where we were baptized together. When I need prayers, she's my prayer warrior.

Seventh grade was a good year for me. I remained good friends with Lindsay, and now I had a new best friend. Beth, Lindsay, and I belonged to a gang of about six girls. We ate lunch together and had sleepovers. I was overall a happy middle-schooler, except that I was being raised by a single mother and an absent father.

Chapter 3

The Surgery
(February 1996)

*You gain strength, <u>courage</u>, and confidence by every experience
in which you really stop to look fear in the face.*

~Eleanor Roosevelt

Amy

In February 1996, I was living in my own apartment and attending college in my hometown. One morning I received a frantic call from my dad's girlfriend. He hadn't gone to work that morning (the first indication something was very wrong) and she found him in his apartment. He had endured a seizure in bed, so violent that he dislocated his shoulders from the force of hitting his headboard. It took doctors very little time to determine my dad's seizures were caused by a massive brain tumor. It had inhabited him for months, but no one knew.

Looking back, we had missed the signs. His writing had turned into scribbles. His headaches had reached epic proportions, and at work, where he was an executive, his performance had slipped in the months leading up to his diagnosis. Sadly, since I had not spent a lot of time with my dad, I had no idea that at only forty-six, he was suffering so much. No one can say how long my dad's tumor had been growing, as he numbed a lot of his pain with alcohol. I remember having several conversations with him, mostly over the phone, when he was drunk. Many of these conversations centered on him trying to figure out how to heal his relationship with Kim, who was still in high school. Whether he used his drinking to numb his physical pain or his mental anguish, I will never know. Perhaps it was a combination of them both.

It was clear that Dad's tumor was so massive that it had to be removed or it would kill him. The doctors scheduled surgery within the same week. The morning of his surgery, I sat in my sociology class. How could I concentrate on my exam, knowing surgeons were drilling into my dad's skull, beginning a long and arduous surgery? I left class, and went to the hospital to sit with my grandparents, my sister, and my two aunts, while we received updates about the surgery every few hours. Things were going according to plan, but there was no doubt it was a complicated task.

I was in a literature class probably not listening—reading wasn't really my thing—when a hall monitor stepped into the room with one of those little pink papers. I didn't get too excited, because I never got called out of class, but then the teacher said *my* name. I knew I couldn't be in trouble, so why was I being called to the office? When I arrived, I saw my mom standing there. She told me Dad had a seizure and was in the hospital.

I remember going into the hospital room and seeing my dad. Terror shone in his eyes, and he couldn't speak. So, I grabbed his hand and told him I loved him. He looked at me and squeezed my hand three times

As my sister and I sat around with the rest of Dad's family listening to doctors and diagnoses, it all went over my head. We quickly decided that surgery was the only option. And it had to be done right away.

The night before the surgery Mom let me lay down with her in bed for a while. My parents were never ones to invite their children into their bed. Even after the divorce, Mom's bed was off limits. As Mom and I lay there trying to make sense of what was happening to Dad, the phone rang. It was my best friend Beth. She wanted to know if I was going to be at the hospital during the surgery and asked what time the surgery was. To my surprise, she said, "I'll meet you at the hospital at 6:00 a.m." I thought she was crazy because she lived two hours away. But, wow, was I glad she did. I really needed her that day! I will never forget running into her arms after they rolled Dad away.

It was a long day. I think the surgery itself took twelve hours. I honestly don't remember how that day ended. We weren't cheering because the surgery went perfectly, but we weren't devastated because of complications either. He made it through. The next day when I came in to visit Dad, his head was all wrapped up like a mummy. A couple of days later his mummy attire was off, and his whole head was exposed. When I arrived, he was sitting up in a chair with his back to me. Thank goodness he couldn't see my face. I think I may have gasped when I saw him. Like something out of a horror movie, the stitches down his head went on forever, and his head was so swollen he looked like Squidward from *SpongeBob*. I took a moment to collect myself, then went in all "Susie sunshine" to help brighten his day. Unfortunately, the days ahead for my dad were not very bright or full of sunshine. Because of the invasiveness of the surgery, he suffered a hemorrhagic stroke, leaving him completely disabled.

Chapter 4

Recovery after Stroke
(February 1996 ~ 2008)

For I am the Lord your God
who takes hold of your right hand and says to you,
Do not fear; I will help you.

~Isaiah 41:13 New International Version

Kim

Once Dad was out of ICU, the recovery process started. He spent over three months in intensive in-patient rehab. Dad's stroke was devastating. He was trying to recover from brain surgery, he was trying to rehabilitate after a stroke, and he was receiving radiation. When I was dismissed from high school at 2:30 p.m. each day, I usually went straight to his rehab center. Since it was on the third floor, and the sign above his door read 3D, we called it 3D rehab. Each day, I parked across the street, walked across Main Street, though the Center's automatic doors, down a hallway, and finally rode up in the elevator. I can still close my eyes and picture this walk. Most days, Dad seemed very happy to see me. For a variety of reasons, I never stayed too long. I had to go to work, do homework, or hang out with friends. In addition, Dad couldn't communicate, and I didn't know what to say. He was always good about kicking me out, too. Probably just so I didn't have to feel bad about leaving.

One day I was off school, so I came in to help him during his therapy. I'll never forget watching a good-looking forty-six-year-old man struggle to put one foot in front of the other. Dad groaned and griped—trying to maneuver his own body was frustrating. My dad, the man who remodeled our house, who was fit as a fiddle, and who was an executive at his workplace, couldn't walk, couldn't talk, and had to use a plastic jug in place of the bathroom. Though Mom kept her distance from what was happening with our dad, she still applied good Christian values when necessary. One day after Dad's surgery, while he was still in the hospital, no one else had time to visit. So Mom put aside all her past hurt and went, serving as an excellent role model for the whole family, Mom cared for him when he was probably at his lowest point. You are probably wondering where that stupid girlfriend of his was, right? Well, she was only around when it was convenient for her!

Amy

I was too young to fully grasp the enormity of what Dad's surgery really entailed—dangerous and risky, not to mention what his stroke would mean for his future. Stroke was something that was associated with old people, or so I thought. Dad was only forty-six. I had no clue what the difference was between an ischemic stroke and a hemorrhagic stroke. For years I wondered why my dad wasn't given the "special stroke drug" to help decrease the deficits he experienced. I was so naïve, I had no idea that the drug did nothing to slow the effects of hemorrhagic strokes. In hindsight, my dad should not have had his surgery in our small hometown in Central Illinois. I don't mean any disrespect in that statement, but Dad's case was so rare and so delicate, he would have been better served to have the surgery performed and his rehab undertaken at one of the top brain institutes in the country. I live with a lot of regret and guilt where my dad is concerned. I wish I would have advocated for him more. However, I have learned that guilt and regret are nothing more than Satan weaseling his way into our lives. I have made peace with my own guilt, but that ugly guilt still worms its way back into my life. I still feel overwhelming sadness. Questions of "What if…?" bombarded my thoughts daily. What if Dad had his surgery at a renowned brain institute? What if he had his rehabilitation at the Chicago Institute of Rehabilitation—a recommendation we ignored because his girlfriend wanted him to stay close to home. What if Kim and I were older, could we have helped him more? What if we had gotten him involved in a stroke support group, would he have felt less alone? The *what ifs* plagued me incessantly, until eventually I felt God tapping me on the shoulder saying, "Enough, Amy. Brad is my child, and so are you."

Shortly after my dad's surgery and subsequent stroke, we learned the tumor they had removed from his brain was indeed malignant. My dad's tumor was called a hemangiopericytoma. I still remember that diagnosis twenty-some years later. A hemangiopericytoma is a rare tumor involving blood vessels and soft tissues. They can originate anywhere in the body where there are capillaries. The most common locations are the brain, lower extremities, pelvic area, head and neck. It is an aggressive tumor. During rehab, Dad not only had to learn how to talk, walk, and use his arm again, but he also started radiation therapy. My self-absorbed twenty-two-year-old self could not appreciate or understand everything he was going through. I was not angry at him during this time, but certainly the relationship between Dad, Kim, and myself was strained before his diagnosis; and after his stroke, we were never able to communicate through words. Sometimes I think that situation was God's way of healing us without words. All the hard stuff was forgotten as we forged forward in helping our dad. As the years wore on, the three of us communicated with each other through our actions and lots of good guesswork. Communicating with Dad after his surgery and stroke was challenging, but he always knew we loved him and supported him.

Dad spent five months in the hospital. During those five months, he went through brain surgery, extensive rehabilitation, and radiation treatment. He came home in July 1996, to his simple two-bedroom apartment. He could walk, but needed a cane. He had no movement in his right arm. His speech remained jumbled and garbled. He had lost all his hair from his treatments and looked like he had spent way too much time out in the sun. If only that were true. His older sister, Susan, came from North Carolina to serve as his twenty-four-hour caregiver for two weeks. After Susan left we all took a deep breath and prayed that Dad could live alone successfully. There were falls, of course, but he never broke anything. He also never spoke another word that we could really decipher. Somehow, he got across the basics to Kim and me.

Once, when I was making a grocery list with him, he desperately tried to tell me he needed toilet paper. After several minutes of utter frustration, he drew a picture of a stick person with a large, round butt and pointed to it. It was like a light bulb went off, "Oh, gotcha, Dad. You need toilet paper!" Dad could be creative when he wanted to be! Humor and laughter were often a much needed and necessary distraction.

Fortunately, Dad had one friend who was incredibly faithful about staying in communication with him. Dad received many cards from this man over the years. This friend would always say to me, "Your dad never deserved this." His heart was in the right place, but it never sat quite right with me because if you're saying one person doesn't deserve something, then does the next person? There are so many things this side of heaven that are hard to understand. Jesus never promised us an easy life. John 16:33 says, "I have told you these things, so that in me you may have peace. In this world you will have trouble. But take heart! I have overcome the world." If I have learned one thing from the hard seasons of my life, it's that this earthly life is not our home. I am certain what Dad went through has an eternal component that I will never understand this side of Heaven. Will there be things that I will ask God once I stand before Him? There was a time I was convinced I would have a laundry list of questions for God, but as I've encountered more difficult seasons in my life, I decided the questions I have from this earthly life won't matter because I will finally be home with my creator.

Several months after Dad had settled into life post-stroke, he expressed a desire to return to work. My sister, my grandparents, and I remained skeptical. Did he really *need* to return to work? His job benefits would sustain him for years following his stroke. We also knew that if the company had a position for Dad, it would not be his former role. Though Dad could no longer communicate verbally, he could drive at least to work. Before Dad's surgery, his neurologist told us she expected him to be back to work within five months. I imagine that might have been true had he not suffered a debilitating stroke.

Nevertheless, we indulged Dad and drove him over to meet with a human resources representative. When my dad, my grandfather, and I arrived, Dad couldn't speak, he was easily confused, his sense of balance was off, and he had no use of his right arm. I wasn't sure what my grandfather was thinking, but I remember thinking the request we were about to make was nuts! However, it is hard to tell someone you love "No" when they just survived life-altering changes. We had to give Dad a chance. We acknowledged that Dad clearly could not return to his former executive position, but requested the company consider placing him in another position—a position that would not require him to speak, a position that would simply allow him to be around other people. We understood it would have to be a position wherein the tasks required very little physically and mentally, but we hoped it would give Dad some sense of accomplishment and provide some social interaction. Though the company was more than gracious to meet with us and the representative treated us kindly, they had no such position to offer. Dad would officially "retire" at forty-seven, declared permanently disabled. Thankfully, he could live comfortably off the excellent company benefits he received.

Kim

Post-stroke, Dad lived independently for fourteen years. At his two-bed-room, second story apartment he was finally able to do daily tasks: getting himself washed and dressed, keeping a tidy home, and fixing himself some-thing to eat. Amy and I usually helped him with groceries, as this was well before the convenience of ordering groceries online. By this time, I was in college. I usually had time in between classes to pick Dad up and run him over to the local grocery store. As we roamed the store buying Fruit Loops, Oreos, and Hungry Man instant potatoes, I would sneak a few things into the cart for myself. I liked to call it my delivery charge. At check-out time, Dad hated waiting in line. Picture this: an old lady slowly putting her wallet away and impatient Dad slowly creeping his cart forward to gently nudge her, silently signaling her to hurry up. When I asked him to stop, he would make some silly face at me. I couldn't help but laugh. All the while the little old lady is still trying to put her wallet away.

Once we were back home, Dad would climb the steps with his cane while I followed with all the groceries. As I unpacked his things, I would unscrew his apple juice, milk, and Listerine lids because he only had the use of one arm. Then it was time to leave. Because of Dad's aphasia, he always said, "Bank ew," which meant thank you. Then he would say, "I wove you," emphasizing you with big puckered out lips. I'd reply, "I love you, too," give him a kiss, and leave.

Chapter 5

Nursing Home

(December 2008 ~ 2018)

Our residents do not live in our workplace. We work in their home.

~Nursing home sign

Kim

As Dad got older, the steps in his apartment grew more difficult for him to climb, so we moved him to a first-floor apartment without any steps. Dad lived a simple life in this gray building with white trim. He liked to leave the sliding glass door open, letting the light come in, and managed to care for the house plants thriving in that spot. Dad watched a lot of TV, comfortable and cozy in his blue leather recliner—shows like *MASH*, *All My Children*, and *In the Heat of the Night*. Things started to change around 2008, however. I remember it was 2008 because I had just had my first child. Dad fell and broke his foot (his first fracture since his stroke). Thankfully, I was already on my way over to check on him, three-month-old Lauren in tow. This was when the family realized he needed help. He couldn't take care of himself anymore. By this time his father had passed and his mother was getting too old to oversee his care, so my aunt became his power of attorney. She also hired assistants to come in a couple of times a day. Before long, we discovered Dad required a higher level of care. So, we hired around the clock help. By December 2009, our sixty-year-old father landed in a nursing home.

Amy,

Making the decision to put our dad in a nursing home was not easy. Our great grandmother spent ten years in a nursing home. Since she lived until 101, we knew longevity ran in the family. We knew the move would be hard on Dad because instead of being in the comfort and privacy of his own apartment, he would now live out his remaining days in a small, confined space with a room-mate. Stroke survivors are creatures of habit. Not only was it hard for Dad to accept this change at such a young age, but it disrupted his schedule and the way he liked things done. Moving Dad into a nursing home was the last thing anyone of us wanted to do, but we needed to keep him safe.

Wanting the best for him, we researched care facilities and finally found the right home. Dad settled into his new situation fairly well. He participated in activities, kept his sense of humor, never missed a meal, and had an entou-rage of nursing home staff—mostly women—who loved him. We often found Dad sitting in his wheelchair, Cubs hat on, in the main entry way. Despite his making the best of his new surroundings, Dad had a hard time accepting that he was as disabled as he was. During his first year living in the nursing home, he lost his mother. My Uncle Kerry (Aunt Karen's husband) drove Grandma to see her son several times during that year before she passed. It must have been heartbreaking for Grandma to visit her son in a nursing home. For her funeral, we hired a nurse to ensure Dad could safely accompany us. It made the day go much smoother for all of us. My Aunt Karen, Dad's sister who was nine years younger, was particularly close to him. I vividly remember watching the two of them at their mother's funeral. Karen stood alongside Dad's wheel-chair. Although Dad could not verbally express himself, I could tell they under-stood each other's feelings as they watched their mother being lowered into the ground, knowing it was their final earthly goodbye. My heart ached because my grandmother was gone, but full of joy to witness the love between my dad and his sister. I always tell my boys there is nothing quite like a sibling. Dad and Karen lived out that relationship. Years earlier, before my dad was disabled, my aunt had endured a very challenging first pregnancy. When she was preg-nant for the second time, she knew she was in store for another difficult nine months. She was on bed rest and every day at noon was her worst time of day.

At that point, her medication had kicked in, which made her feel lousy, she felt sad, and the weight of the entire pregnancy seemed to overwhelm her. So, my dad called her every day at 12:00 p.m. to get her through it. He drew on his greatest attribute, his sense of humor, to generate laughs. He also told Karen stories until he could sense his sister smiling, confident she felt better, giving him the peace of mind he needed until he called her at the same time the very next day. We all celebrated when Aunt Karen gave birth to another healthy girl.

Kim

After a stroke, people often experience physical, emotional, and behavioral changes. Thankfully Dad never got depressed, or at least he didn't show it to us. He occasionally seemed anxious or angry, however. I would describe it more as frustrated at times and uneasy about certain situations. When he lived on his own, he didn't leave his apartment much. He thrived on sticking to his routine. He seemed very content in his new life, but it was very different from his old life. I pride myself on having a great personality and being the life of the party—most definitely a trait I inherited from my father. It's not that he lost this, he just wasn't around people much anymore. I guess that was the one bright spot to moving him into the nursing home. Everyone loved Dad! Watching someone suffer from a stroke is heart-wrenching, but also inspiring. I am really proud of how my dad accepted the hand he was dealt, lived life despite the odds, and still managed to make people smile—which is pretty impressive when you can't communicate! Even though nursing home life consisted of bland meals, a warm climate, a slight smell of urine, except on hair day (that's when all the ladies got their perms), and the occasional scream or moan from random residents, Dad seemed satisfied. He was like Fonzie at Al's Diner, except he was Bradford of Heritage Manor. The residents and staff all called him Bradford, which I loved. No one had ever called him by his full name before. Sometime I brought him communion from church. We sat together and prayed. Even though he couldn't pray with words, I knew he still had a relationship with God. When I finished praying with him he always proudly said, "Amen!"

In 2011, Dad's last grandchild was born. My uncle picked him up from the nursing home and brought him to my driveway. We could not maneuver Dad up my front steps, so I brought my little four-pound bundle of joy out to the car so he could hold the baby. I can still picture how Dad's eyes lit up when I placed Luke in his arms.

Years later I would trudge into the nursing home with Lauren in tow and Luke on my hip. Eventually, Lauren would beg to push Grandpa in the wheelchair and Luke would ride on his lap. Dad only had one working arm, but he always did a great job holding on tight to my kids.

During one visit, I arrived to find Dad sitting in the main lobby chatting with a visitor. I was so excited that someone had come to see him, I went right over to see who it was. The woman said her name was Susan and she was visiting from Atlanta.

Several months prior, this woman had emailed Aunt Karen saying she used to work with Dad and wanted to come visit. My aunt had no idea it was the woman with whom my dad had his first affair in 1983! So of course Karen gave Susan his address. After Susan flew into town, she even had dinner with my aunt. The next morning, Susan met Amy when they both visited Dad. Amy had no clue who the lady was, so she treated her very nicely. Later, when my sister told me about the visit, I asked some questions, and finally, the light bulb went off. "Amy, you dumb ass! That was Dad's mistress!"

Months after this encounter, Susan returned for a second visit, and met me. As I walked into the home, there she was, wanting to shake my hand! I took my hand away as if to psyche her out. I took a step back. My face reddened to the point of explosion, I announced in the meanest voice I could muster, "I can't even stand to look at you!" With that, I spun around and walked out, pulling Lauren by the hand. My little three-year-old was so confused.

"Mommy, why we go? I want to see Grandpa."

"We don't like that lady, we are mad at Grandpa, and we are leaving, come on!" I replied, dragging her behind me.

All the way home she kept repeating, "We no like that lady."

"That's right, Lauren. We don't like that lady."

I was so angry that even after all those years, the poor decisions my dad made during the '80s were still coming back to bite us. It took me three to four weeks to recover enough to visit my dad again.

Amy

Kim's description of meeting "the other woman" is funny, and I can tell you that's exactly how she reacted when she met Susan. It's true that when I met her, I didn't put two and two together. I was just so thrilled that someone had come to visit my dad. I do remember Dad doing a lot of eye-rolling while the three of us chatted. I wondered what the heck was going on, but eye rolling with Dad was not that unusual. After Kim's encounter with Susan, she never returned. The biggest question I had from that entire ordeal was, what did my dad mean to this woman and what did she mean to him? Was he the love of her life? I was really struck by the fact that over twenty years had gone by, yet she bought a plane ticket and stayed in a lonely hotel room for a few days just so she could visit her broken-down former lover, who now lived in a nursing home. Had the affair gone on longer than anyone knew? After the dust settled, I asked my dad about Susan. Unfortunately, his verbal skills had deteriorated so much by that time even his yesses and no's were unreliable. As the years went on, Dad's mobility declined, and he spent his days in bed or in his wheelchair. On his good days, Kim and I brought him out to our homes for an occasional visit, but once he became completely wheelchair-bound, I found it impossible to transport him ourselves. December was always the hardest month for all of us. Another Christmas in the nursing home would come and go. My friends, Kim, and I organized "Socks for Seniors" where we collected socks for the residents. A few days before Christmas we passed the socks out and sang songs. For many years, Dad seemed to enjoy this fun event. He wore a Santa hat and we pushed him around the home while we spread good cheer. There was one particular year, however, he seemed annoyed by the event. That was when Kim and I decided to call it quits. It seemed that Dad had reached his limit. In December 2017—his last December here on earth—he appeared particularly sad. In a desperate attempt to lift his spirits, I decided to take him for a car ride. Dad's face lit up at the suggestion. Due to the challenge of getting him in a car, I hadn't taken him for a car ride in years. Bless the nurses on that cold winter day! Despite the snow, they expertly managed the lift machine to get Dad settled in my car. He smiled like a kid in a candy shop. I took him to get a milkshake, which he promptly spilled on the floor of my car. He hung his head in embarrassment, and I told him the milkshake was nothing compared to all the junk my boys had spilled in my car—which made him smile.

Life holds unforgettable moments. For so many reasons, that December day was one of them. When we returned to the nursing home, the nurses stood waiting to help Dad out of the car and safely into his wheelchair. The receptionist at the home had appeared when we returned. She was a dear lady who always asked my sister and me about our kids, and she thought our dad was hilarious. As we rolled Dad past her desk, she had tears in her eyes. "In all my years of knowing Brad, I've never seen him taken out of the home," she said.

This kind woman never intended to hurt me, but boy, she sure did. Those words cut me to my core. In that instant, I knew I had failed my dad. I let his disability get in the way of my time with him. I returned to my car, crying (and I'm really not a crier), feeling so much shame and guilt, wishing I had handled things differently with him.

Kim

Here's the thing about Amy and me. We are always on the same page. We share many of the same feelings (guilt, sadness, anger) when facing a situation. This is how our relationship works. When one of us is feeling a certain way, the other one puts things into perspective for her. Amy's feelings of guilt for not taking Dad out more serve as a case in point. I would say, "Amy, don't feel that way! You have to remember that for years we *did* take him out and about. However, he never wanted to be anywhere for long. Being out of his routine for too long was hard for his stroke brain. He would get uncomfortable or antsy and demand to go home. Poor Aunt Karen had to leave halfway through my wedding because he wanted to go home! Also, no one at the nursing home ever offered to help us take him out, and we couldn't maneuver him safely. Not to mention that we were working moms trying to do the daily grind, and didn't have hours in our day to take dad on a drive. So, there you go, Amy, no more feeling guilty!" Then Amy would say, "Yes, Kim, you are right." To which I replied, "I know, I'm always right." One thing I have learned in adulthood is that shame and guilt are wasted emotions. These feelings don't benefit anyone.

It's the devil's way of inching his way into our lives. Unfortunately, I have not perfected the art of eliminating my guilt or shame either. I guess that's why God made us sisters. If we have to feel this way, at least we can do it together. Amy shared her story with me, and I too went over to the home to bust Dad out of there. It took two nurses, a very interesting lift contraption, and about twenty minutes to get him into my car. I stood off to the side watching two lovely ladies get Dad all hooked up. They hoisted him up from the ground, where he hung in the air like a giant baby in a baby swing. Once we were settled in the car, Dad grabbed my hand with pure joy in his eyes. I got out my phone and took a selfie of the two of us. Little did I know that would be the last picture I took with Dad.

Chapter 6

Final Days
(March 5~15, 2018)

The pain you have been feeling can't compare to the joy that is coming.

~Roman 8:18

Amy

On March 3, 2018, I hosted a birthday dinner for Mom to celebrate her sixty-seventh birthday. The family enjoyed dinner, with lots of laughter and conversation, which is typical for our get-togethers. The next day brought weather beautiful enough to open the windows—a rare treat that time of year in Central Illinois. My husband, our boys, and I cranked up the music while we ripped up our old carpeting in anticipation of the new flooring my husband planned to install. The four of us ate burgers together, excited about another home project completed. It was the kind of weekend where I went to bed on Sunday night with a thankful heart, praising God for the health and happiness of my family. Then, at 2:38 a.m. on Monday, March 5, Aunt Karen called me. The call woke me out of my blissful sleep. Karen served as Dad's power of attorney, and it was not unusual for the nursing home to call her during the middle the night, which then prompted a call to me. I had not had a middle-of-the-night call about Dad in several years. This phone call changed everything. It's funny how life can change in an instant, and it's always the things you don't see coming— like Karen's call—that hit you the hardest. Karen explained that Dad was being rushed to the ER. She asked if I could meet him there. I wasn't worried, even though Dad's health had declined in the previous year. Recently, he had troubling swallowing, but he was still eating. We assumed his swallowing issues resulted from his neurological decline. He also spent a significant amount of time in bed, sleeping. My aunt's conferences with the nursing home hadn't revealed any red flags or causes for concern. But tonight Dad woke up vomiting blood. I decided to meet Dad in the ER before calling my sister. I wanted to give her a few more hours of rest. I figured Dad had accidentally bitten his tongue, and he would be back at the nursing home in time for breakfast.

When I arrived at the ER, Dad was bright-eyed and just as confused as I was. The staff checked the inside of his mouth. They noticed a dark, coffee color to the dried blood, but he was no longer actively bleeding. He immediately failed a swallowing test, which meant he'd receive no food or water. He was admitted to the hospital. We could swab his mouth with a wet sponge, and he was made comfortable with IV fluids. The staff explained that after twenty-four hours his hunger pains would dissipate, though this brought little consolation to my sister and me. On Wednesday, March 7, Dad was taken for an endoscope to see where the bleeding was coming from. The doctor said it was hard to even get the scope down his throat because of a very large tumor growing at the base of his tongue. Even though I was then forty-three-years-old, I was living in la-la land. I surmised that just because he had a tumor, it didn't mean he had cancer. Certainly it could be removed without disrupting my dad's life.

I was getting ready for work Monday morning, March 5, when I got a text from Aunt Karen. Dad had thrown up blood, and Amy spent most of the night with him in the ER. God love my sister, because she knows how much I love my sleep.

At the time, I was in my sixteenth year of teaching. I taught fourth grade at an elementary school only a few blocks away from Dad's nursing home. I called Amy, made sub plans, and went straight to the hospital. Amy and I didn't realize that day signaled the beginning of the end for our father. We had no idea we would spend the next ten days balancing work, family, and tending to our ailing parent. Anyone who has ever experienced such a crisis is all too familiar with the delicate balance of caring for a loved one while trying to handle a job and a family at the same time.

During Dad's hospital stay, I struggled most with getting answers. I felt that the doctors were not giving us much information. How could we know what to do and what treatment he needed without clear information? No one could tell us if the tumor was cancerous or if it could even be removed. We only knew for certain that they could not get a scope down his throat. After his CT scan, we still had no answers. I tried to get whatever information I could from his chart, but unfortunately, I had no idea what heterogeneous meant, what a glossopharyngeal sulcus was, or if 5.6 cm was big or not. My good friend Katie called or texted daily to check on me, helped me with my kids, and was very supportive. But, I felt most grateful for her honesty. She had a good amount of medical knowledge. She was able to tell me that the tumor was big and that it was most likely cancerous.

One evening when Lauren and I were visiting Dad, we experienced an unpleasant surprise. Lauren sat happily playing with her toys, while I rubbed Dad's feet with lotion. (It was definitely an act of love, because Dad's feet were awful!) All was going well when a very nice woman with long hair and a sweet smile came into the room. I'm a pretty friendly person, so when she approached me, we immediately started chatting. Suddenly, the conversation took an unexpected turn. Words like comfort care and hospice started to float from her mouth, and I started to freak out. The family hadn't even been told what the mass under Dad's tongue was or if we even had a treatment plan. I asked her to stop talking. I wasn't comfortable having this conversation without my aunt or my sister. The hospice social worker dialed Karen, and I got on my phone with Amy. Now, all three of us continued to listen to this woman together. I don't really remember everything that was said, but I do clearly remember the message that Dad's chances of dying were pretty high. When Karen and Amy left the call, the palliative care representative smiled, handed me a business card, told me to call with any questions or concerns, and left the room. I got up, stood by Dad's bed, took his hand, and asked if he understood what was happening. I tried to reassure him by telling him I loved him. He mumbled something nearly indecipherable, but I knew exactly what he meant: "I don't want to die."

Amy,

We decided that in order to figure out what was going on Dad would need to have an endoscope to see where the bleeding was coming from. My sister was there with Dad when he came back from the procedure. He was a mess. He had an allergic reaction to the dye contrast. He was bruised all over from the IVs. He seemed very agitated with the nurses. For the past twenty-two years, my Dad's body had let him down, and this time was no different. Within twenty-four hours after the endoscope, hospice came into Dad's room to talk to the family. Sadly, I was not there. I went home to work for a few hours. I was blessed with a work-from-home-job, but during this time it was a delicate balance, and Kim and I found it very difficult. While I was trying to catch up on work, Kim called me and put me on speakerphone. As the hospice worker spoke, I kept thinking, *I cannot believe this. Are we really at the point where hospice is involved?* We didn't even know if Dad's tumor was benign or malignant. That evening our Aunt Karen, Uncle Kerry, and Kim met in the hospital to discuss what to do. Discussions about a loved one's care are never easy, especially when that loved one cannot advocate for himself. You question whether or not you are making the right decision. What were we dealing with? What was the treatment? It's heartbreaking! My dad knew his situation was dire. We wanted to make whatever time he had left on earth filled with love and dignity.

Aunt Karen, Kim, and I immediately decided we needed to find out if my dad's tumor was cancerous, which meant he had to undergo a biopsy. Maybe, just maybe, the situation wasn't as doom and gloom as we thought. But Uncle Kerry spoke up. I will never forget his words, and I will always be grateful to him for speaking the truth with all the love he always held in his heart for Karen, Kim, Dad, and me. He asked the three of us why we wanted to put dad through yet another procedure. After all, hadn't Dad's body been through enough in twenty-two years? Could we really expect a different outcome? It was the "ah-ha" moment we needed. So, we opted to start hospice, which meant he would be discharged from the hospital and sent back to the nursing home to live out his last days. Though we faced a heart-wrenching decision, afterward I felt blanketed in peace—which I can only say came from God. God gave us a big God wink the next day. After the ear, nose, throat specialist examined Dad (we were not present for this exam), he called my aunt and very boldly stated that he made it a point to not get involved in family decisions, but in my dad's case he confirmed that our family was absolutely doing the right thing. Dad's tumor was more than likely cancerous, and the treatment for it had more risks than rewards: it would weaken his body even more and produce no guarantees. Dad's quality of life was already poor, so further procedures and treatments would certainly annihilate what little he had left.

Even in the midst of such sadness, I could see God's light shining through all the brokenness. After everything Dad had been through, I felt unprepared to see him leave his earthly life. Death is never fun. During this time all I had to hang my hat on was God's promises to us. Dad remained a believer, and my sister and I clung to Romans 8:18 (the pain that you've been feeling can't compare to the joy that's coming).I witnessed God at work, and I felt His presence daily. It started with the well-intentioned doctor who affirmed our family made the right decision. We saw God's presence in the tears of the nursing home director who met with Kim and me at the hospital before we brought him back to the nursing home to die. She said it would be an honor to care for him in his last days. After all, he had been a resident there for many years and she truly cared about him. I saw God in the gift of time. Each and every day my sister and I were given the gift of time.

Since our aunt had committed to caring for her granddaughter during the day, she couldn't come to the hospital. So she often made evening trips to visit her brother. My sister and I adore our Aunt Karen, like seriously adore her, but God saw to it that our dad spent his final days with his daughters. We spent day after day together, just the three of us, laughing. Yes, in the depths of utter sadness we laughed. The laughter brought us all great joy. This precious time reminded us of the dad of our childhood, and it warmed our hearts. We remembered how he rolled his eyes at the nurses behind their backs, and they had no idea why we were laughing. But Dad *was* dying. The day Dad was discharged from the hospital and transported to the nursing home Kim and I were a nervous wreck. We knew we could not be with him 24 hours a day, seven days a week. We again saw God in the nurse who greeted us the night Dad came back to the nursing home. Through her tears, she assured us, it was her honor to care for her patient of nine years.

The biggest God wink came five days later. Dad was admitted into the hospital and we knew he was dying. I had signed up to take a test for work that I could not cancel. If I cancelled I would have had to reimburse my employer hundreds of dollars. In fact, this was the last day I could take the test without incurring those fees! I was in no condition to concentrate, but I had no choice. Somehow, I took the test and passed, which I can only say was an act of God. As I went to check out after my test, a woman printed off my exam grade because I had passed, she complimented me and told me it was a great way to start my day. I said I was glad I passed, but I was headed to a meeting with a hospice nurse to discuss plans for my dad.

The woman smiled warmly and commented how hospice workers are such special people. She told me she only worked at the exam center one day per month. She also shared she was in ministry. After a brief silence, she said something that blew me away: "You tell your dad the best is yet to come." It seemed no accident that she was working on the day I took my test; this woman had to be an angel sent by God to comfort me. She told me she had died briefly when she was fifty-five but been revived. While dead, she experienced Heaven. She said it was indescribable and amazing. To that very day, she felt as if she was in a shell and did not belong in her earthly life. She reiterated again to me that there was nothing else like it. I sat listening to her in awe. She told her story with such simplicity and calmness, but very matter of fact. With tears in my eyes, I walked out of that exam center knowing without a doubt God had placed this woman directly in my path to give me the peace and comfort I so desperately needed.

Kim

During this incredibly sad time in our lives, I too saw God's light. I felt God's warmth and love, and I heard Him speaking directly to me.

"Wait patiently for the Lord to be brave and courageous.
Yes, wait patiently for the Lord."

~Psalm 27:14

I'm a planner. I have a busy schedule and a strict to-do list. I found dealing with hospitals, doctors, and hospice hard to fit into my already hectic life. Once the idea of hospice set in, I struggled with decisions such as, do I take off work, how much work can I miss, and how long will Dad be dying? I wanted someone to tell me, "Your dad will be gone five days from now," which no one could say. If death had any certainty, I would not have worked or left Dad's side.

One thing that no one tells you about death is how painful it is. Not so much for Dad, he was very doped up. I made sure of it. I mean for me. It's a sick feeling in your stomach that doesn't go away. It's an ache in your heart that you can't explain. It's a lump in your throat that takes your breath away.

As I was reading my devotional one day, the reader had written, "Don't let the pain speak louder than God's love for you. The pain you bear can have meaning by bringing glory to God. Don't concentrate on pain. Instead be bold in your patience for the lord." God sent another messenger to ask for my patience. Another verse that helped me was Proverbs 19:21, "Many are the plans in a person's heart, but it is the Lord's purpose that prevails." This is one I live by now. I always have plan A, B, C, and D. But guess what? I'm not in charge; God is. God would call Dad home on His schedule, not mine.

Amy

When we elected to start hospice, all of the tubes and IVs that were connected to Dad were terminated. He was relieved on the day he saw his last IV come out of his body. He got to wear regular clothes and we made him as comfortable as we could. He went back to the nursing home to spend his final days. The last few days of his life were beautiful. Kim and I hold those days as sacred, but they were also the hardest days of our lives. When hospice began, Kim and I met with nurses, pastors, grief support people, and honestly, as the days wore on, it was a blur. I couldn't believe we had reached this point. In all honesty, I thought when it was my dad's time that God would just take him in his sleep. I knew my dad's body had worn out, and it was time for him to go home. Looking back, I recognize how God used Dad's final week as a way for the three of us to reconnect, to repair and heal any old wounds.

On the morning of Wednesday, March 14, another hospice nurse came to examine Dad. After her visit, my sister and I asked her how much time she thought he might have. She thought he would get through the week, but would more than likely pass over the weekend. Overall, his vitals were good, and she fully expected him to have a few more days ahead of him.

Kim and I used every minute we could to be by Dad's side. We prayed with him. We talked to him, and we laughed with him. We also discussed with our aunt that we did not feel we needed to be present for his death.

I know there are a lot of people who wait until everyone is out of the room to pass. Since Dad could not communicate, it was impossible to know what he wanted. My aunt helped guide Kim and me in our decision. We knew it could be days before he passed, and we still had families and jobs to manage, which made it impossible for us to be with Dad twenty-four hours per day.

At noon on March 14, just a few hours after the hospice worker examined him, Dad shut his eyes and his breathing grew very labored. He never opened his eyes again, but we knew he heard us and felt our presence. That evening when Karen came to visit, she sent us home for some rest. Anyone who has watched a loved one die knows the emotional toll it can take, and after nearly twelve hours of sitting by Dad's side that day, we needed a break. That evening we had requested a hospice volunteer to sit with Dad until midnight. We were thankful for those sweet volunteers who relieved Kim and me.

At 12:30 a.m. on March 15, my phone rang. I heard my aunt's voice on the line. "Is he gone, Karen?" "No," she replied. She explained that Dad's nurse from the home called to say he only had hours to live. I admit, I didn't know what to do. Selfishly, I didn't think I was strong enough.

I praise God that he gave Kim and me the courage we needed to be by our dad's side, and I am so very thankful for his nurse that night. I picked Kim up, and with knots in the pits of our stomachs we drove to the home. I prayed repeatedly during that drive that if we were not meant to be with our dad for his passing, God would take him before we arrived. When we arrived at Dad's bedside at 1:00 a.m., we clearly saw Dad had waited for us. He needed his girls with him as he journeyed from this earthly life to his forever home.

When we grabbed his hands, he immediately relaxed. We comforted him and told him we would not leave his side, that we would be here to send him home, into the arms of Jesus. I repeatedly said the Lord's Prayer. Kim and I told him it was okay for him to go home; we would be just fine. Around 2:00 a.m., he received his last dose of morphine. We kept talking to him knowing that hearing was the last sense to go. Kim and I told Dad how much we loved him, and in that last moment, I told him that we knew he loved us. As Dad took his final breath, Kim and I held each other over his bed and wept.

Kim

There were so many times during this experience that I did things that I never thought I was strong enough or competent enough to do. Before we left the hospital to return to the nursing home, I felt hopeful that we could just stay in the hospital. The hospital room was spacious and had plenty of seating. There was no way I was going to sit in that tiny hot nursing home room, where there was no seating, to watch my dad die next to his roommate. Well, I spent five days in that stifling room sitting in a lawn chair. Looking back, God did give us the gift of time. Those last days were joyful. One special memory I had was when my cousin brought her baby in to meet Dad for the first time. My dad was a great uncle and had a special place in his heart for Michelle and Kelly. When Michelle came around that corner holding Jocelyn, my father's eyes lit up as he reached for her. When Michelle placed her in his dying arms, I watched with tearful eyes as he smiled in awe of this sweet baby.

God also gave us the gift of special people. One morning I got up early so I could check on Dad before I went to work. As I love to sleep, 6:00 a.m. is really early for me! Dad was happy to see me, and before I left, he told me he loved me. As I walked out of the nursing home, I wondered how many more times would I hear him say "I love you." When I got to school, the halls were still dark. I walked down the hall feeling like a robot. I knew my legs were moving, but I didn't know how.

A sweet teacher's aide passed by. She said, "Are you okay?" I fell into her arms crying. "No." She held me for a bit, then I told her my dad was dying and this might be the last time I would hear him say "I love you." I was grateful to this woman for her kindness that day and it was probably good for me to verbalize what I was feeling instead of just going through the motions. Then

I wiped my face, thanked her for the hug, and went into my classroom to get ready for my day. I pulled myself together, knowing I had a standardized test to give to my students. I took the afternoon off, however, to be with Dad. Not only was he awake and alert, he must have said, "I love you," at least ten more times.

In these last days, Amy, Dad, and I truly did enjoy each other's company. One afternoon, in particular, I asked Dad if he was comfortable and if he needed anything: water, a foot rub, a beer? When you are caring for someone who is dying, you just want to make them comfortable and happy. When I mentioned beer, Dad perked right up and said very clearly, "Yes!" I turned to Amy and said, "Well, get the man a beer!" She was shocked at my absurd idea of giving our dad beer. Her reply had something to do with not mixing alcohol and morphine. I reminded Amy that it wasn't like he was going to be driving a car or operating heavy machinery. What was it going to do, kill him? Amy, of course, rolled her eyes and agreed, but worried about sneaking it into a nursing home. Amy always had to make sure all the "boxes" were checked before we did something.

So I got the three of us a six-pack. Dad was so proud of me and thrilled when we turned on Kenny Rogers' "The Gambler." We poured beer into a cup, soaked up some Miller Lite onto the stick sponge for Dad, and put it in his mouth. Talk about pure joy. He quickly motioned for more. We toasted, laughed, sang, drank, and just loved each other.

During this time, I read a lot about the process of dying. I had two very good friends who were nurses. They spent a lot of time talking to me about what to expect. I have always been grateful for everything they shared with me and the hours and hours of support that they gave me.

My friend Katie was at her grandfather's side when he passed five months earlier. Once I knew Dad was dying, she offered to come into the hospital to trim his beard. She said it would be an honor to give Dad his last haircut and that's exactly what she did.

As the days passed, I allowed my kids to come see him until it seemed inappropriate. One afternoon, my daughter Lauren brought her grandpa a little stuffed wolf she won from school for being good. He loved it. My dad always loved stuffed animals. That day was the last time they saw their grandpa.

That same night I was very concerned about his congested breathing and the fact that he had not eaten or drunk anything except that sponge beer in over six days. Katie offered to go in with me to take his vitals and give me her opinion. When we got there, Dad was happy to see us. He remembered Katie from when she came to cut his beard. He was still holding onto that little wolf Lauren had given him.

It was really cute when Katie reached to get his hand to get his blood pressure. Dad thought she was trying to take his wolf. He snatched that thing away from her and gave her a look to kill. We laughed as she explained she was only there to take his blood pressure, not steal his wolf.

We did finally manage to get his vitals, which were pretty good. His blood pressure seemed a little high due to the near wolf-napping. God bless Katie for being with me that night, for easing my mind, and for having a good sense of humor. The next day would be the last day I would see my father alive.

On March 14, I went to work for a few hours. Then over my planning period, I went to see Dad at 9:00 a.m. He was awake, but he was not doing very well, and he felt cold. Amy was there with me. When it was time to go back to school, I struggled to leave. Thankfully, Amy stayed. I walked out to get into my car, but I physically could not open the door. I called work and said I couldn't make it back that day. At one point I wondered how Dad was still alive. He was so fragile and hadn't had any food or water in days. What was he holding out for? That's when I called Mom.

Amy and I struggled with this. We were not positive what Dad wanted, and we really didn't want to put Mom in an uncomfortable situation.

One of the things I have always admired about my mom is her selflessness, forgiveness, and kindness. For years she visited Dad in the home at Christmas so that we could be with our families. She always said, "I'll do whatever I can to help you girls." So, when I called, she came.

On Wednesday afternoon Dad fell unconscious, but we could tell he knew she was there. We stood back and watched our teary-eyed mother take our father's hand. "Hi, Brad, it's me," she said. "As I was driving over, I thought to myself what am I going to say to you? And then a song came on the radio: Blood, Sweat, and Tears ' 'You make me so very happy.'"

She asked Dad if he remembered, but of course he could not answer. We all knew he knew the song. Mom held Dad's hand and sang out, "You made me so very happy

I'm so glad you came into my life
You made me so very happy
You made me so, so very happy, baby
I'm so glad you
Came into my life."

Thank you, Mom and Dad, for showing us how to love.

Aunt Karen and Uncle Kerry came to the nursing home around 5:30 p.m. They both encouraged us to go home and get some rest. They would stay with Dad for a few hours. I remember struggling with leaving, but hospice staff told us Dad might hang on several more days.

Uncle Kerry took my face in his hands, "It will be okay. It will be okay. You can go home."

So, I wiped my teary face, hugged him, and went home. I felt sad, heavy, and lost. I laid awake a little while with these thoughts and then drifted off to sleep. The phone rang at midnight. I picked it up and said, "Is he gone?" Amy said, "No, but he is in his last hours." Sobbing, my husband tried to console me as I dressed. Down the hall, Lauren was sitting straight up in bed.

"Did Grandpa die?" she asked. I hugged and kissed her. "No, not yet. But I'm going there now to help him get to Heaven." Amy came to pick me up, and we sat in my driveway and prayed. When we got to the nursing home, we walked down the dark halls trembling. A place that was always well-lit and full of people was dark and somber. We held tight to each other's hands as we entered Dad's room.

His bed was low to the ground, and there were pads on the floor in case he fell out of bed. Amy rushed right over, got on her knees, and told Dad we were there. I stood there, frozen, taking in the awful sound.

The death rattle is the most horrific sound I have ever heard. The sound of someone's body shutting down, drowning in its own fluids. I stood there next to the curtain, my dying dad on one side and his roommate on the other, and emotion took over.

I left the room bawling, unable to breathe. I paced the hall for just a minute, took a deep breath, and went back to my dad's room. I got on my knees next to him and recited the Lord's Prayer. The next hour was painfully hard. There were a couple of times I heard what I thought was his last breath, though it wasn't. Amy told Dad he would forever live on in my sense of humor, Jay's good looks, Nick's work ethic, Lauren's affectionate nature, and Luke's silly faces. We told him to go home and reminded him that we loved him over and over. When we finally changed our wording and said, "We know you love us," he took his last breath. It was his way of saying I love you one last time. I felt God in that room, and as soon as he was gone I knew Dad was in heaven.

Nobody wants to talk about what happens after a loved one passes, so I'll share it with you now. Dad's nurse came in to declare him dead. He called the coroner, answered a bunch of questions, and then we signed some papers. All the while, with a dead guy just lying there.

I recalled the lady at Amy's testing center who referred to her humanly body as a shell. That was exactly how I saw Dad at that time. He was already with his heavenly father, and what remained on earth was just a shell. As Amy and I packed up a few of Dad's things, I felt aware that he wasn't here anymore.

We exited the dark nursing home exactly two hours after we had walked in. We pushed a cart that had a blanket, a few pictures, and a bunch of baseball hats. We looked at each other and said, "This is it; this is all we have left of our dad." My minister preaches on this often. He says we come into this world naked, and we leave this world naked. The "stuff" we have doesn't matter. This rings so true. The verse that I clung to during this time, and still do, is Romans 8:18. "The pain you are feeling can't compare to the joy that's coming. I am comforted knowing my father is bursting with joy in the kingdom of Heaven."

Just a couple days after Dad passed, Katie stopped by one morning to share a dream she experienced. She debated about telling me, as she wasn't sure how I would react. She dreamed about her grandfather for the first time since his death. She couldn't see him, but she could hear him clearly. She called for him, "Gramps, Gramps." Katie continued to call for her gramps when all of the sudden he had a message for her, "Tell her he's here, tell her he's here!" Katie kept calling for him but he was gone. The "her" he was referring to was me, and the "he" was my dad. Katie felt sure of it. Amy, Katie, and I all shed some happy, thankful tears. This is just one of the many things I love about God. He works in ways we don't expect and answers us when we need Him most.

Chapter 7

Mom

She opens her mouth with wisdom.
The teaching of kindness is on her tongue.

~Proverbs 31:26

Kim

When Dad moved out, and Amy went to college, it was Mom and me against the world. I loved being with my mom, spending time chatting, playing games, doing life—just me and her. I not only thought she was cool, but I was in awe of her. She never felt sorry for herself or showed any anger about living as a newly-single woman. She focused on me, but not in a co-dependent, I-can't-live-without-you way.

Mom also worked to become her best self. She probably owned and read twenty self-help books. Amy and I used to make fun of her. Now I feel bad. It was probably a good thing she read those books. Instead of falling apart, she took what life threw at her and made the best of it. She even went back to school to pursue her master's degree. I remember several summers when Mom got on her bike and pedaled all the way across town to the university for an early-morning class. She arrived back home around noon just as I was getting out of bed in time to fix me lunch. Then she spent the rest of the day carting me around to activities. She encouraged me to get my lifeguarding certification, so in the dead of winter after teaching all day, she trucked me across town to my classes for three hours, five days a week, for eight weeks. Now that I am a mother of two kids who teaches all day, I can appreciate this! When I got my first lifeguard job, she drove me across town to work until I turned sixteen and she could loan me the car.

One day I forgot my frozen dinner at home, so she kindly brought it over to me so I wouldn't starve. When she arrived, I happened to be around the corner on my cigarette break! I had an unfortunate smoking habit my mother knew nothing about. When I saw her walk up, I knew I was caught! I stood there in shock, as a frozen Lean Cuisine hit me right in my forehead. She aimed it perfectly at my head, it hit me hard, and she just turned and walked away. It was actually quite impressive because she was standing pretty far away from me. I had a bruise! The rest of my shift, I was a mess. What would Mom say? Would I be grounded? Once I got home, I got the "I'm so disappointed in you" lecture. I hated disappointing my mom! I wish I could say I decided right then and there never to smoke again, but sadly, I did not.

During my high school years, Mom had dinner waiting on the table every night after swim practice, and we would eat together. Our favorite meal was baked potatoes with cheese and extra butter. She also got up extra early the next morning to get me to 5:00 a.m. swim practice. She also knew how important vacations were to us. She got us to Virginia Beach with the help of her brother Mike's directions. And this was before cell phones and GPS. She also flew us to Destin, Florida for spring break. One time, when we hit turbulence, I threw my Dr. Pepper all over her yellow outfit. She never made me feel bad about it. She just walked around with soda all over her, which if you know my mom is a really big deal. She likes her clothes to look nice! The funny thing is that Mom still talks about that flight as the worst ever, but now we can laugh about it.

When it was time for me to go to college, I didn't go far. I spent my first year at a junior college only forty-five minutes away. I spent most weekends at home because my friend Beth went to the university nearby. In my final years of college, I was sick of roommates, so I moved back home, and Mom and I we were a dynamite duo again. This time it was just fun. I had gotten all my bad girl nonsense out of my system, and was getting serious with a nice guy (my future husband) who lived two hours away. So, Mom didn't have to "mother" me. We just got to be companions, friends, a perfect mother-daughter pair. Mom and I did everything together: wedding planning, walks, dinner, shopping, and teacher stuff. I was in my first year of teaching, and Mom was in her fifteenth.

When I moved out in June 2003, we continued to spend time together, just not as much. My new house had a pool, so she came and paddled around with me. We met for walks and still talked on the phone daily. She finally retired when her youngest grandchild, Luke, was a baby and her oldest, Jay, was entering fourth grade. When I had my children, she helped me with after-school care and did fun activities with us. She loved having her "grands" come stay with her. She only wanted one at a time, so she could focus all her attention on that child. She worked very hard spending time getting to know each grandchild individually and building a beautiful bond with each one.

As I aged, my job got harder. I always dreamed of being a teacher. I did it, and I did it well. I loved my co-workers, and I loved the kids—even though they were at times very challenging. As the years went by, the work got harder and my life got busier. I had a hard time managing and balancing everything. Mom was always good at giving advice and helping me through life. But around 2016, we started hitting a rough patch. We had what you would call a "disconnect." Looking back, I think my issues had to do with feeling very criticized by Mom. She had a rough several years with her parents and then lost both of them within five months of each other. And then felt like she lost me too because of our disconnect. If I could go back, I wish I would have been there more for her and been more flexible. I have always wanted to be the perfect daughter, a daughter my mom could be proud of. Unfortunately, at this time in my life she made me feel like she didn't agree with the decisions I made or how I was running my life. When she would say things to me, I would immediately take them as criticism. I don't know if that's on me for taking things the wrong way and being overly sensitive, or on her for digging at me because of how she was feeling. I imagine it was probably a little bit of both. I was distancing myself from mom and pushing her away because I didn't want her advice. I wanted to do things my way. I believed I no longer needed her help; I had things figured out. In reality, what I ended up doing was hurting her. I no longer made her a priority, and I shut her out.

Amy

Mom is fiercely independent and loves to travel. She is an avid book reader, an active church member, has a tribe of girlfriends, adores her four grandchildren, and lives to seize the day. She loves to take trips. Once her girlfriends called and asked if she wanted to take a trip to the Jersey Shore. Mom thought about it a few days and concluded she had the finances to do it, she was healthy, and she would enjoy it, so she went. She ended up having an awesome time.

Mom is always fully aware of how precious life is. Often times I would call her and she would pick up the phone and tell me she was praising God. He had blessed her with good health, a home she loved, two daughters, and four grandchildren. With all that, how could life get any better? There was one thing, however, that was a thorn in Mom's side—her diabetes. Mom was diagnosed with diabetes twenty-one years earlier, when she was forty-six years old, which unfortunately became type I. We've been told she has a "rare case" for an adult. No matter how much weight Mom lost or how good her A1C was, the highs and lows were a constant battle for her. During one trip with friends, Mom's blood sugar dropped so low they had to call 9-1-1. In November 2017, after eleven months of watching her weight, Mom reached her goal weight. She was the healthiest I had ever seen her. She was moving better, eating better, and she felt very satisfied with her life. She also took care of herself and her disease. Mom's faith is the foundation of who she is. As our story evolved, God was at work with His perfect timing. Sometimes the timing was hard to swallow, but as He led Kim and me down the path we were walking, we were able to see His plan more clearly. Relationships were restored and strengthened, and our Mom's amazing faith was witnessed first-hand. Even after Dad's passing, his presence was interwoven with ours, especially after her stroke.

Chapter 8

Something Is Wrong
(July 9, 2018)

Yes, even if I walk through the valley of the shadow of death,
I will not be afraid of anything, because You are with me.
You have a walking stick with which to guide and one with which to help.
These comfort me.

~Psalm 23:4

Amy

I work from home, and Mom and I usually chatted several times a day. One day when I took her call, I was greeted with silence. I knew Mom was on the line, because I could hear her breathing. My heart started to race. Was her blood sugar low? When her blood sugar went low, Mom got easily confused. "Mom, are you okay?" I asked, feeling more frantic with every passing second that she didn't answer me.

"Amy, something is wrong," I finally heard Mom slur. I immediately knew Mom was having a stroke. I hung up the phone, raced out of my basement office, and into my driveway where I knew I'd have better cell reception. Panicked, I called Kim, who lives only five minutes from Mom and could get to her faster. Then I dialed 9-1-1. Somehow, I calmly told the operator my mom was having a stroke. Then I called Kim back, and we agreed to meet at the hospital.

It was a normal summer morning for my kids and me. I was preparing for swim lessons, busily gathering towels and goggles. Mom had planned to meet us there. When the kids and I arrived, she was already there, waving and smiling at us. She had on a pretty green T-shirt and white leggings. Mom looked cute even when she wasn't trying. We sat and chatted while watching the kids swim. After swim lessons, Mom needed to go run her errands. I waved, said goodbye, and told her I would call her later. There was no indication that Mom would suffer a massive stroke two hours later.

My daughter Lauren and I were headed across town to her flute lesson when I got the call from my sister. I heard Amy say something, but the call dropped, as it usually does because she lives out in the middle of nowhere and has horrible reception. But I could hear a panic in her voice.

Something was definitely wrong. I frantically ran into the flute lesson, grabbed Lauren, and tore down the street like a bat out of hell. My whole body shook with fear. I pulled up to my mom's house and literally sprinted inside, which fat girls really don't do! I could barely feel my legs moving under my trembling body. I stopped directly in front of her, out of breath, put my hands on my mom's knees and said, "I'm here." She tried to talk but couldn't. I could see the fear in her eyes.

The paramedics arrived and worked fast. I got into the ambulance to ride to the hospital with her. In the meantime, I texted close friends to start praying. I had a hard time catching my breath, because fear had taken over my body. I'm not even sure I could blink, either.

At the hospital, the ER staff immediately took Mom for a CT scan. I paced the hall, waiting to see what would happen next, and waiting for my sister—who had at least a thirty-minute drive—to arrive. I took deep breaths, put my hands together, and prayed. I prayed so hard. I prayed that Mom would be okay. I prayed for the medical staff. I prayed for strength and comfort.

Amy,

Arriving at the hospital and laying eyes on mom, I was pleasantly surprised by what I saw. She was sitting up in a bed, completely coherent. The right side of her face seemed somewhat droopy, and her speech was slurred, but she could move her right arm and her right leg. Then the questions began. When a person has a stroke, the medical staff quickly determines whether to administer the life-saving drug Tissue Plasminogen Activator (TPA). It can be very effective in reducing the life-long deficits that strokes can produce, but only when given within three hours of the initial stroke symptoms. Thankfully, Mom was well within the time limit. After receiving TPA, the doctors then needed to determine whether to keep Mom at the local hospital or transfer her to St. Francis Medical Center in Peoria, IL, which had a neurological intensive care unit. Kim and I wanted Mom transferred to Peoria (we definitely wanted to make better decisions than we had with our dad), but the transfer decision was out of our hands.

As we awaited the care team's decision, Mom's dear friend, Leslie, showed up. The three of us held hands and prayed. Leslie asked God to place Mom at the hospital that could best treat her. Minutes later, the medical staff announced they would be taking Mom via helicopter to Peoria! As I drove forty-five minutes to the new hospital, I felt calm, almost stoic. My mind remained remarkably free of "what ifs," or "whys," or even fear. The stroke seemed a minor bump in the road. Mom had received TPA, and surely that would do its job.

My feeling that everything was going to be okay was confirmed when I was the first to arrive at the Neuro ICU. Mom had been taken for her angiogram procedure to remove a blood clot that had ingrained itself into her brain. Her nurse was giddy, saying Mom was in such good shape that she probably would not require any therapy. I pictured taking Mom home from the hospital that very same week. Strokes may get some people down, but surely not my mom.

I will never forget the first forty-eight hours of Mom's hospitalization. Kim and I camped out at her bedside while a nurse came in every hour to "quiz" Mom. They would ask the same questions over and over again: "What is your name? Why are you here? Do you know what day it is?" I held my breath every time, hoping and praying Mom would speak clearly and answer the questions correctly. It was painful to watch, because all Mom wanted to do was sleep. During several of these hourly tests, she refused to wake up. Then the nurse had to decide whether Mom was suffering another stroke or simply exhausted. This situation resulted in her undergoing another CT scan.

That CT scan reflected a possible brain bleed or perhaps another stroke. Because doctors were unsure, they treated Mom for a possible brain bleed by lowering her blood pressure. With that action, we risked another stroke, but it would help stop the bleed. Kim and I must have looked like deer in headlights at that news. I was even too shocked to pray.

Ironically, when Mom's friend left the hospital, we were all smiles, praising God that doctors had gotten her clot out, and she was doing so well. It's amazing how drastically Mom's situation changed within three short hours. My sister and I had to depend on each other and God during that long, hard night, the wounds from our dad's death four months earlier still painfully fresh. The thought of losing our mother seemed incomprehensible.

Kim

After finalizing things with my kids, I packed a bag for Mom of things I thought she might need. I was under the impression that Mom was doing great, and I anticipated she would be home in a few days. When I arrived at her room in the ICU, Amy was super optimistic about Mom's prognosis and reiterated what the nurse had told her. I felt instant relief.

As with most things in life, there's good and bad about being an ICU patient. The good is that nurses usually only have two patients to worry about, so they are always checking in on the patient and the family. The bad thing is there is no seating in an ICU room. I understood hospitals don't want to overwhelm the patient, but Amy and I were not leaving our mother's side. So, we sat on two folding chairs with about as much padding as a teenager's bra. I remember one particular moment when I propped my feet up on one chair and sat in the other and leaned my head against the wall and closed my eyes. It was the first time I had closed my eyes in over twenty-four hours. They didn't stay closed for long because in came a nurse with a barrage of questions: "What's your name? Do you know where you are? Who is our president? What's your birthday?"

After Mom tried to answer the questions, she endured the motor test. She had to push her feet up towards her head, then down towards her bed. She had to pull her arm towards herself and away from herself, which she could barely do. Hour after hour, Amy and I watched Mom try to complete these simple tasks. She did okay at times, but through the night we saw a steady decline. I remember one particular time when she was alert enough, but only slurred her name and barely moved her arms or legs. Her eyes rolled back in her head, and she laid her head back on her pillow. I sat there and watched my mother with complete shock. I couldn't believe that just four months after my dad's passing I had to watch another parent struggle after a massive brain injury. As she slurred words, I thought to myself, I cannot possibly endure not communicating with my mom. I spent twenty-two years silently communicating with my dad. Why was this happening to us?

As a result of Mom's decline, doctors ordered another CT scan. By the time we saw the sunrise, Mom had a total of four CT scans in a twelve-hour period.

Amy

As we entered day two of Mom's stroke situation, my feelings of calm were overtaken by crippling fear. She underwent multiple CT scans because doctors suspected a brain bleed. We were told that nothing could be done for a brain bleed. Mom was a brittle diabetic, which was a big contributor to her stroke. How in the world could she recover from this and still manage her diabetes?

For years my sister and I joked that God wouldn't allow Mom to suffer a stroke because surely our dad's stroke was enough. But when it did strike us twice, I think we were too shocked to react. Fear and worry became an all too familiar emotion.

I've since learned that in a way, we were testing God. We weren't doing it intentionally, but that's exactly what we were doing. As a Christ follower, you don't test God, you trust Him. When tragedy struck initially, Kim and I had a hard time trusting God's plan. Would our mom suffer the same fate as our dad? Would she ever utter another word that we could understand? Would she be able to live independently and manage her diabetes?

Kim and I worried about the obstacles ahead of us and Mom. We watched our dad walk with a cane for years. He never got back the use of his right arm. Would Mom's arm hang the same way? Would she struggle to get her coats on and off as much as Dad did? Would we have to get her groceries, as we did for Dad for years? The worry seemed all encompassing. We had so many unanswered questions, but God always prevails. Although I know this is true, for the first forty-eight hours of Mom's stroke, my faith was shaken to its core.

One morning, I was driving to the hospital when my friend Mary called me with a very clear message. At that very same time, Kim's friend Karrie was relaying the exact same message. Satan had wormed his way into our mom's health crises. He was making us believe there was no hope. He was trying to destroy the faith we had in Jesus. Our weakness was his opportunity to strike. Every fear, doubt, and concern we had, Satan wanted to amplify it. I couldn't believe it hadn't occurred to me that Satan had his hands in our situation. I was simply so overwhelmed I couldn't see it.

When Kim and I met at the hospital that morning, we literally ran to the chapel, got on our knees, and asked Jesus for forgiveness for not trusting him. We grew confident He would steer us through Mom's recovery. God has total authority over Satan, and we prayed him out of our situation, in Jesus' name. At that moment I could literally feel Satan leave. Poof, just like that, the crippling fear was gone.

After we prayed together in the chapel, we prayed over our mom, giving her encouragement and hope. That day was a turning point for us. No longer would we let Satan place unimaginable fear in us. It was like a dark force dissipated, letting the light shine through. That same day we finally got answers, answers that gave us hope. Mom did not have a brain bleed. She did not suffer a second stroke. She had survived one (although massive) stroke, and TPA had helped her.

Mom started to talk that afternoon. She passed her swallowing test, and she could move her right leg—all very encouraging signs. When the doctor spoke to us that afternoon, he said, "Be patient. Give your mom seventy-two hours, and see what she does." Patience was an attribute I'm certain that God wanted to instill in all three of us, as none of us is very good at it.

Kim

Satan made us believe there was no hope for Mom's situation. He was trying to destroy the faith we had in Jesus, knowing full well Amy and I trusted Him, even though I was angry with Him. When Amy and I prayed together in that chapel, it was the most spiritual moment of my life thus far. Amy took my hand, and we prayed Satan away. She reinforced our trust in Jesus. We knew He would heal our mom. No longer would we let Satan control our thoughts. That same day, we finally got answers, answers that gave us hope. Mom did not have a brain bleed. It was dye from the contrast of the CT scan! What happened that day was a miracle. God is real, and God is good!

Those first forty-eight hours were a blur of emotions, mostly fear. During hard times, I always leaned on God and prayed for His help. As each hour passed, and things got worse, I got mad—very, very mad! How could God do this to us twice? Standing over Mom's bedside seeing her completely debilitated, unable to speak I wanted to scream. We did this already! We just buried our dad four months earlier after watching him suffer from the effects of a stroke for over twenty-two years! In that moment I hated God. After we received the news about the bleed, the doctors cleared out, and Amy and I went into the hall in complete shock and silence. We were basically being told our mother could be a vegetable, and only time would tell the outcome. Amy and I were motionless. We stared at each other, then fell into one another's arms crying. Through her tears, Amy said, "I don't know how to put one foot in front of the other without our mom." My heart was breaking and the hurt crushed me. I knew the road to recovery would be long and hard.

I remember praying for God to take Mom home if it wasn't in His plan to heal her. I didn't want Mom to have to go through what Dad had been through. Amy and I were fully aware of what Mom's wishes were. She would never want to continue with this earthly life if she couldn't be productive in it. I felt we had two options; a miracle or a peaceful death. How could I bear to lose my mom, and how could I bear to see her debilitated? It was so painful to imagine either one. Thankfully, we didn't have to.

Chapter 9

Rehab

(July ~ August 2018)

The human spirit is stronger than anything that can happen to it.

~C.C Scott

Kim

At the end of seventy-two hours, three days of lying in a bed, I was glad to see that someone was going to get Mom up. It took two therapists to maneuver her, not because she was big, but because her body did not work. We said a million times thank goodness Mom took off some weight. Mom was excited to get up, but once she was out of bed and on her feet her expression changed. Her legs were on the ground, but she couldn't support herself. I can't imagine what that must've felt like for her.

Mom's spirits were not great at this time, so it didn't help that seventy-two hours after her stroke, she was barely able to speak. Mom loved to talk. She had a fluent vocabulary and prided herself on being a great communicator, so this was frustrating. Her speech improved over time, but it was very difficult for her to produce a thought, let alone a sentence. I patiently listened or asked for clues. She'd try a few times, roll her eyes, and close them, as if to say, "never mind."

As we moved forward, Mom remained very cooperative and worked hard to improve. She made progress, though it was made in baby steps.

After Mom was stabilized it was time to start the recovery process. I could see things were starting to get better. After days of heart-wrenching fear, I finally felt that everything might be okay. My spirits were lifting but our unknown future still gnawed at me. Mom still had a lot of rehabilitation ahead of her, and it was still unknown if she could live independently; so this is when I decided to take a year leave of absence from my teaching job.

Amy

Kim made Mom a poster with "Baby Steps" written across it. Always the artist, she made small footprints on it, and every day we wrote Mom's progress inside them—no matter how small. The physical therapist set goals for Mom, and she surpassed them. If the therapist wanted Mom to walk one step, she walked four.

Speech remained very challenging. Mom knew exactly what she wanted to say, but the words wouldn't come out. The day-in, day-out of the entire process was exhausting.

Kim and I attended nearly all of Mom's speech sessions. I admit I was, selfishly, most concerned with Mom's speech. Mom's language was a huge part of her identity. She and I spent countless hours on the phone each week. She has a fluent and wide vocabulary. She loved to read. Her two book clubs gave her great joy. The other selfish part of me didn't want things to play out for her like they did for Dad. Not having language skills limits a person. It closes one's world a little bit at a time, and I knew it would crush Mom.

One night before Mom started rehab, she insisted we go home and get some rest. She hadn't ordered dinner yet, and we went over the menu. I offered to order her meal for her, but she insisted she could do it. We practiced dialing the phone and rehearsing what she wanted from the menu. Bound and determined, sure enough she did it.

Little by little her speech came back, but it took time. During one session early in her rehab, she had trouble saying easy words like "pig," "goat," and "dog." I sat in that session, put a smile on my face, and tried to look encouraging, but I was dying inside. I wanted to scream at God, "For all the love, this woman was an English teacher! Make her speech fluent again!"

Before Mom's stroke, she called me every day at 9:30 a.m., right after she got home from water aerobics. I missed those calls, where she told me about her flowers and the new clothes she found to fit her new slim figure. It hurt knowing that for a while most of Mom's favorite activities—like book club, water aerobics, traveling, church, and spending time with family and friends— all had to wait. Right now, Mom's life was very limited. I thought of her every morning knowing that she needed to pee, she had to wait for a nurse to get her out of bed. Next, she'd endure a crappy cup of hospital coffee—sad, because she loved her morning coffee.

Even so, Mom rarely complained. During rehab, the only thing mom ever complained about—and I use that term loosely—was the nurses taking her vitals at the most inopportune times. Mom, Kim, and I have great respect for nurses (many of our dearest friends are nurses), and we understood the nurses were only doing their jobs. It was hard on Mom once she fell asleep to be woken up (every four hours) for a vitals check. But, during this time, Mom's spirits were good, considering her life changed in a blink of an eye. She tackled each day with grit, determination, strength, and faith.

Kim had such faith during this time. She remained confident Mom would be restored one hundred percent back to her former self. I wasn't so sure. It wasn't that I didn't have faith—trust me, during this time it was all I had—but I had been down this road before, and I just wasn't sure how much restoration would be done. Every time I heard Mom's broken speech, every time I saw her struggle to take a step, and every time I saw her arm hang from her body, I remembered that Mom's recovery would be long and require extraordinary patience (something Mom and I aren't so good at).

One of our biggest struggles during this time was the bathroom. Mom and I have bladders the size of a shot glass. There is nothing wrong with us, but if we even look at water, let alone actually drink it, we have to pee…constantly. Thankfully, Kim didn't get cursed with an inefficient bladder! Kim and I had to get "green lighted" by the staff in order to help Mom with transfers from bed to the toilet, and she needed to go to the bathroom six times per hour—no joke! The bathroom was a vicious cycle: Mom wouldn't want to drink because she'd have to pee, but if she didn't, it affected her diabetes. The situation greatly improved once Kim and I received the "go ahead."

Kim

When Mom was well enough to leave the ICU, she was moved to a private room with a great view of a big beautiful church with two giant steeples next to the river. When I looked at it, it seemed I could feel God's arms wrapped around me. I was feeling good about Mom's new room and thrilled to have her out of the ICU.

After Mom was all settled into her new room, I left for the night planning to come back early in the morning to help her with bathroom, shower, and breakfast. The next day I pulled into the dark parking garage at about 6:30 a.m. Much to Amy's surprise I arrived earlier than her most days. I always wanted to see how Mom's night was and to help her get to the bathroom. As Amy said, our poor mom suffers from having to go to the bathroom all the time, so not being able to walk or get out of bed was frustrating. One morning I had a good feeling about how well Mom was doing. The elevator dinged. I hopped off and marched straight into Mom's room I noticed it was dark, which was unusual because my mom is an early riser. As I got closer to the bed, I thought, *Geez, mom looks awful.* As I got even closer, I not only thought she looked awful, but hairy too! That's when I realized I was looking at a man! I immediately headed to the nurses' station demanding to know why a man was in my mom's bed. Mom had switched rooms again!

Here's the thing about brain injuries: doctors and nurses are always assessing the brain function and continuously checking patients several times a day. In those first few days, whenever a doctor or nurse would come in to assess Mom, I was unable to take in the magnitude of what had happened to my mother, the fact that she lay there unable to do easy tasks. But as the days inched on, I saw little by little her brain started to work again. She shrugged her right shoulder a bit. She stood assisted. When a doctor asked Mom who I was, she looked at me, then looked at the doctor, then said clearly, "Daughter Kim." Music to my ears! She wrote a phrase "grandgirl Lauren." She asked me about the fruit in her fridge (which my kids already ate). She asked me to get a book from her house and even told me where it was. Eventually, we played rummy. Slowly but surely, things were improving.

My mom is like me in that she loves the sun. One day I got permission to take Mom outside. There was a patio that could be accessed from the hospital, but it would take some work because much of the hospital was under construction. I ventured off to find a suitable patio spot while Amy did crosswords with Mom. It turned out that Mom's brain post-stroke was still smarter than both her daughters'! She got all the words way before Amy did. After going through what felt like a rat maze, I found a spot. Amy and I wheeled Mom out to the patio, and we all soaked up the sun for a few minutes. It was a much needed few minutes of normalcy.

Many days I felt like I had a part in the movie *Groundhog Day*. My days consisted of waking up, going to the hospital, coming home, trying to play catch up with my kids, and maybe getting a little sleep. My family really struggled during this time. My daughter Lauren was ten, and my son Luke was seven. They really needed me at home, but my mother needed me more. My husband, Craig, is a wonderful father and husband and did what I asked, but the truth is I run the show at home. I maintain the structure of the home, set the rules, and make sure everything runs smoothly. If you are the head of your household, you know how demanding this can be. This was a very stressful time on me and my family. Thankfully, it was summer, so I was off. But for my kids and me, summer is always pools, play dates, and fun. This year, our plans were horrifically interrupted by Mom's stroke. Although my kids understood what had happened to their Nana, they did not fully grasp the severity of it. Once she was out of ICU, they visited and thought Nana was doing great. She was, but only the adults understood the long road ahead of her.

One day when I took the kids along to the hospital, they got to see their Nana do physical therapy. Luke followed behind her with the wheelchair as she held onto the parallel bars and walked a few steps. Every time the therapist would ask, "Sue, do you want to take a break?" Mom would sweetly reply, "No, let's keep going." She worked so hard, and her right leg was getting much stronger. After visiting with Nana for a bit, I decided to take the kids to the Peoria zoo. This was something Mom and I enjoyed every summer with the kids. Although both of us were sad we couldn't continue the tradition, Mom and I both knew how important it was for me to go with them. They had been shuffled back and forth between grandparents and neighbors for several weeks already. I took lots of pictures and videos, so we could show Nana what a great time we had during our visit.

Amy and I observed Mom's slow-but-steady progress every day in rehab. The hardest part of all was watching Mom feel so defeated. She just wanted her body and voice to work. One day about half way through rehab, I realized my mom was superwoman! She started her day by having a nice conversation with me. It was really hard for her to communicate, but she was able to take my hand and tell me that I was being wonderful to her. We then proceeded to talk about my future career goals, and she was able to give me advice. Teaching is something Mom and I always had in common. Later, during physical therapy, she wore some bionic contraption called an exoskeleton. It hooked onto her body and helped her walk like a robot. Even though she rolled her eyes and hated the whole thing, she worked hard and was able to stand for twenty-eight minutes and walked 215 steps in eight minutes. During speech therapy, we played a game, kind of like heads up, except with flashcards. She was able to describe over ten words that I had to guess. Then she guessed all the words I described. During occupational therapy, a therapist worked on her right arm the whole hour. He used a simulator to make the muscles move. Her arm reacted—a good sign. She had some shoulder movement, but still no elbow or hand movement. Then the therapist put her on her belly to bare weight on that arm. This task seemed very difficult for Mom, but she stayed focused and worked hard. In my mind, she made me so proud that day! I knew she would get through rehab, she would communicate perfectly, and her body would work again, because she was our superwoman! Sometimes Amy and I would get discouraged that Mom would never return to her "old" self. I would watch her try to talk and walk, with her arm just hanging there. It made me worried about the future. I feared Mom might be unable to care for herself, or she could fall, or worse, she might become more debilitated. When all these worries came into my head, I read Ephesians 6:16: "In addition to all this, take up the shield of faith, with which you can extinguish all the flaming arrows of the evil one." I am the Lord's faithful servant, I thought, and the fiery arrows—such as worry, fear, anxiety, and stress—will *not* get me! Sometimes things felt unattainable, but then God reminded me he *was* healing my mom—itself a miracle. I had a front row seat to her amazing recovery. I remembered that most people don't even survive a stroke like Mom's, and here she was thriving.

Amy

One evening while Mom was still in intensive care, four of my dearest friends came to visit me. At the time, Kim and I took shifts at night. Since sleeping in an ICU waiting room is far from ideal, Kim bought me a sleep mask so I could actually get some shut eye there, usually making do in a reclining rocker. (Nobody knows sleep better than Kim!) The night my closest friends showed up, I was running on nothing. The only time I could remember feeling that tired was during my boys' first six months of life. My memory is foggy, but I think my friend Jenny texted me and said she and our friend Sarah were coming to visit, and asked me if I needed anything. I was too tired to formulate a sentence, let alone make any decision as to what, if anything, I might need. So, I told her "nothing," and I warned her not to expect much from me. I felt like the walking dead. My sister and I were in the waiting room around 5:00 p.m. when Kim spotted them. She nudged me and said, "Amy, they all came!" I looked up, and there were my four closest girlfriends—Jenny, Sarah, Mary, and Shannon! Each of them carried goodies in her arms. They brought me a warm meal with a warm cookie as a bonus. I didn't think I was hungry until I devoured that meal. They had also packed an overnight bag filled with toiletries and clothes—all things I had failed to pack for myself in the craziness that ensued after Mom's stroke.

Sadly, my friend Shannon was also familiar with strokes, so she was a great comfort to me, providing advice and encouragement. Mary and her husband made me meals after Mom got home, and Mary's husband John, who has one of the biggest hearts, continues to provide physical therapy for Mom. Jenny and I still say how thankful we are that she was here during my mom's health crises. Jenny and her family had lived in Mom's house a month prior to her stroke, while they were preparing for their move to Texas. It was a move that was difficult for our families. My generous friend Sarah is one of my mom's biggest cheerleaders and helped me clean her house before she came home from rehab. She was and still is helpful with anything I ask of her. Mostly my friends made me laugh and they gave me comfort during a time when I needed them most. That night I took a much-needed shower and had everything I needed thanks to my wonderful friends!

Chapter 10

Home and Beyond

(August ~ September 2018)

The best way to find yourself is to lose yourself in the service of others.

~Gandhi

Amy

Mom went through many changes both in rehab and after she came home. Getting Mom home and settled was harder than Kim and I anticipated. Although Kim was not working, she had two little kids at home who were being shuffled between her mother-in-law and our friend Katie. Thankfully, my oldest son had his driver's license, so it did take some of the pressure off of me. But I was still working, and my husband ran his own business, so I never knew what his schedule would be. We knew Mom would need twenty-four-hour care when she came home, and we naively thought that we could assign care-giving shifts to Mom's friends. The reality was, Mom was most comfortable with Kim or me taking care of her. She was already trying to adapt to getting comfortable with being uncomfortable. Kim and I did not want to add to her stress, so we assigned ourselves to the round-the-clock shifts. I won't lie: by the end of those shifts we were going crazy! I was convinced that if I had to watch another episode of *Garage Sale Mysteries* on the Hallmark channel, I would come unglued! Thankfully, I kept vodka in the fridge and made sure I had a nightly cocktail. Mom was truly agreeable, and you couldn't ask for a better patient, but she was trying to adapt to the changes in her own life—one of which was having her daughters live with her.

Kim bought a sensor that alerted us if Mom got out of bed at night. Though we wanted to give mom her privacy, she wasn't quite capable of walking herself to the bathroom at night. As soon as she swung her legs out of bed, the sensor beeped loudly. Talk about a wake-up call! Since Mom had to go to the bathroom several times during the night, I would just start to fall asleep and "beeeeppp!" Another monumental change we all had to adjust to was Mom's new insulin pump. Mom's recovery was good, bad, and ugly. The good was her recovery was going quite well. Her mobility was coming back, her speech grew less broken, and even her arm showed some movement. The bad was her diabetes continued to frustrate all three of us. The ugly part of Mom's story was the pump. It was just that—UGLY! Stroke survivors don't like to do things outside of their comfort zone, and asking a stroke survivor to learn something new is challenging. Mom wasn't crazy about the pump before her stroke, less so after her stroke. The pump was a disaster. I never fully grasped how to use it. Mom seriously hated it. Kim mastered it, so most of the burden of the pump rested on her shoulders. We needed to push the button about ten times per day, and we had to change the injection site every three days.

As the days went on, Mom was very thankful for our help, which she obviously needed since she was at such high risk for falls. Amy and I helped her practice walking. We stood close by with our hands held out to catch her like a mother chasing after a toddler learning to walk. Every time Mom misstepped, I would gasp and reach out. She grabbed onto me to catch her balance. She sustained three or four falls—like Dad—and thankfully she never got hurt.

We also worried about Mom breaking her single functional arm. I remember one fall she sustained because she tried to push in her dining room chair. Mom has always been a visual person. How things look has been very important to her. She likes things orderly. And that is how she kept her house. So when the chair was out of place she wanted to fix it. I was sitting in the living room and rushed over to her in a panic. My heart raced because we couldn't bear having to send her to a nursing home. I told her to lay still, asked what hurt, and then talked her through how she would get up. We talked about how she had to let some things go. She didn't listen very well, because her second fall revolved around trying to straighten a rug. How hard this time must have seemed for mom! Although she couldn't even do small tasks—like pushing in a chair or fixing a rug—she never let it get her down. Mom's attitude, for the most part, always stayed upbeat. She tired easily, but always worked hard on her recovery. She has always been very goal-oriented, so she didn't spend much time thinking "poor me," she just persevered.

Since I was Mom's primary caregiver, we spent a lot of time together in the first few months after she came home. Sometimes it felt grueling—not because she was a difficult patient, but because of unexpected sensor and pharmaceutical issues, and Mom's obsession with changing her closet. Although she always maintained a positive attitude, at times her new life as a stroke survivor was hard and emotionally draining. Sometimes Mom had a rough day. She was, after all, entitled to one. Overall, I enjoyed my role as a caregiver. There were certainly many funny stories along the way.

To help keep her safe, I ordered Mom an alert system. The necklace has a button you push, and it calls your selected first responders with a prerecorded message, "I've fallen and I can't get up." Mom was "thrilled" to have this new device—NOT! I programmed Amy's, my husband's, and my phone numbers into the device. Once I set it all up, I checked to see if it was working. I pushed the button, and right away my phone rang. I was so proud of myself! I felt good about this purchase, knowing it would make us feel better about leaving Mom alone. I went to sit down and put my feet up, congratulating myself for a job well done. Then I looked out the window to see an ambulance in the driveway. I ran out apologizing telling the EMTs. I didn't mean to call them! When I explained the whole situation, they were very kind and even joked about how I could go to jail for calling 911 for a non-emergency. Ha ha, funny, not funny! When they asked to come in and check out the system, one of the medics decided to go into the room where Mom was sleeping. She was surprised by her wake-up call. "They are not here for me, right?" "No, Mom, they are here because of me!"

Mom's speech blunders provided us with a lot of laughs along the way. In the fall of 2018, her speech had improved, but she still struggled with getting words out or coming up with the right word. One day she said she wanted to eat a piece of tsunami cake! I laughed and corrected her, "Tiramisu cake." Also,

Mom's right hand remained a little swollen. She wanted to ask the occupational therapist about it and struggled to explain the problem. It came out, "I am fat hands." Thankfully, the OT immediately understood and gave Mom a compression glove. I called it her Michael Jackson glove! Mom uses that glove to this day when she struggles with her "fat hand." Obviously, Mom's limitations frustrated her. A few times she told me she felt so old since her stroke. I quickly replied, "Mom, you're not old, you're just a little brain damaged!" We laughed. Humor got us through many challenging times. Every day we would look for something to laugh about, and we always found something.

Chapter 11

Stroke #2

(September 26, 2018)

Jesus replied, "You do not realize now what I am doing,
but later you will understand."

~*John 13:7 New International Version (NIV)*

Kim

Once we cut back on 24 hour care and the kids went back to school Mom and I settled into our new schedule. I would get to her house between 6:30-7:00 a.m. I would help her with breakfast, getting dressed, chores, and then we would get ready to go to therapy or swimming. We usually ran errands together after therapy. Mom would often say, "I'm just so happy you are here with me," or, "What would I do without you?" I wouldn't skip a beat with my response; I'd tell her she'd be screwed! Swimming was always our favorite. Mom always did water aerobics at her local health club before her stroke, and we wanted to keep that up. Plus, it was a great way to do more therapy. I got a caregiver badge and went with her. We usually went at least twice a week. All of her water friends were so delighted to see her and welcomed me like I was one of them. I used to make fun of Mom for doing water aerobics, but I ended up being the one in the water bouncing around the water and loving it! After swimming, I would usually stay with her, make her lunch, and get any tasks done and then be home by 2:00 p.m. to get my kids off the bus. In the evenings, Amy or a friend would bring in dinner and be with her for several hours. Once she was ready for bed, we left her alone at night with a bedside commode. Then I would do it all again the next day. I would pull in about 7 a.m. to get her newspaper, open the garage, walk up the driveway, and I would usually find mom sitting watching *Good Morning America*. This daily routine lasted throughout the fall, and by Thanksgiving, Mom was needing me less, which was a good thing!

One day in late September, I got to Mom's around 8:00 a.m. because we didn't have therapy until 10:00. I grabbed the paper, walked up the drive, and entered the house. It was still dark. I immediately knew something was wrong. Mom never sleeps past 7:00. I entered her room and she was in her bed, unresponsive. I tried to shake her awake. Her eyes were glazed over and they had rolled back into her head. I immediately grabbed her blood monitor and learned her blood sugar was over 500! Her insulin pump had stopped working during the night, and at that time, we did not use a diabetic sensor. Amy and I had no idea her blood sugar had reached such an epic high level. I calmly called 911. The hardest part was when the paramedics were taking her out of the house. She was very nauseous and was moaning and wailing. I just kept reassuring her that I was there and she would be okay. The ambulance doors closed and I dropped to my knees and sobbed.

Amy,

I know Kim will always live with the image of finding mom unresponsive that morning. There have been times when I thought Kim might be overreacting to things with Mom, but I always try to give her the benefit of the doubt because I wasn't the one who found her that September morning. During Mom's hospital stay, she underwent yet another series of CT scans and MRIs, and it was determined she indeed had a second stroke. It was much smaller than the first but it was very close to her language center. Before that September morning, Mom's speech was so good she had been released from speech therapy, two weeks prior to her second stroke. Another stroke meant she would be back in speech therapy. However, it did not affect any of her mobility. We were so thankful for that. As disappointing as that second stroke was, I was once again reminded that we were not alone. God was still in control and this was another bump in the road, but He was at work. For a few weeks prior to Mom's second stroke, she had fallen into an abyss of depression. My mom never battled depression. There is no shame in depression or taking meds to help with depression. She had started medication after her first stoke and then decided to go off of them, which is what caused the decline in her mood. Thankfully, after several rough weeks she agreed to go back on them. I personally found it very hard to watch my mother fall into the deep dark depression hole, not knowing how I would possibly pull her out. Once again Mom's dear friend Leslie prayed. We surrounded Mom's bedside while she remained unresponsive. Leslie prayed that Mom would be better in the morning, and she asked God to restore her emotional state of well-being. Then Mary's mom, Joyce, who I personally think has a bat phone to God, stayed up all night on September 26, and prayed for Mom. When I came into Mom's room on September 27, she was sitting up, smiling, and talking (broken, but we could understand her). And she laughed. Have you ever loved someone and witnessed them fall into a depression? Most people have, but the greatest gift is to hear true laughter come from your loved one. I don't want to make light of this situation because there are many people who pray to God for years that He take away their depression or their addiction, and nothing happens. I don't think we prayed any harder than anyone else. I also don't think God hears us any more than He hears others. There are some things we won't know or understand this side of heaven. Hearing Mom laugh, Kim, Leslie, and I surrounded Mom's bed, and through our tears we laughed with her. Then on September 27, Mom confessed to us that she was praying again. Mom had stopped praying for a time period, not because she was mad at God or doubted Him, but because she was overwhelmed and, honestly, her brain wasn't functioning properly. The day after Mom's second stroke, things just felt different. I believe it was God's intervention to get our attention, which seemed nuts, as if the last six months wasn't enough to get our attention; but I think God continues to move in our lives so that His children can keep moving and changing in the way He desires for us. Perhaps it was God's way of helping Mom accept where she was and reminding her that He is in control.

Kim

Since Mom and I had been planning a trip to New York (way before her first stroke), it was very clear once she had been hospitalized for the second time that we would not be going!

Mom and Amy had taken a trip to Texas back in April, three months before Mom's first stroke. Mom and I wanted to take our mother-daughter trip to New York just as she and my grandmother had done years ago. On July 5, just four days before her first stroke, I had booked our entire trip. A beautiful hotel in Times Square, right in the theater district because we would be seeing three shows; *Kinky Boots*, *Beautiful*, and *Mean Girls*. All three booked! After Mom's stroke, I wasn't sure if we would be able to make our trip. However, once I saw that her recovery was going so well, I thought maybe we could go—until the second stroke happened, and it was clear God did not want us going to New York. I was devastated. I had a dear friend call to check on me as she did weekly even though I sometimes wouldn't respond. But this day I did, and she offered to help cancel everything and get refunds. I took her up on her offer and was grateful for her doing this for me. We may or may not get to New York but that's okay. We are blessed that our mother is here on this earth, able to enjoy most everything that she used to. We ended up doing an overnight in Chicago and seeing the show *Charlie and the Chocolate Factory*, which was excellent and adorable!

Amy

As 2018 came to a close, I was sound asleep in Texas. My family had taken a trip to see our dearest friends who had moved six months earlier. We missed them like crazy and it was another change I was trying to adapt to. Kim, Mom, and I were well-aware of the blessings in 2018, but we were all glad to see it from our rear-view mirror. As we entered 2019, Mom was doing so well, but it had taken us months to get to that point, to be able to say to people, "She's doing awesome!" One of the greatest joys from Mom's stroke was witnessing how God used all of my sister's strengths. I think for several years before the stroke, the three of us got pulled into the craziness of life, which is filled with disappointments and hurt feelings. Kim and I have very different families, very different jobs; and as we aged, I became more introverted and Kim got more extroverted, all factors that didn't cause any brokenness or unkindness in our relationship, but more of a disconnect. All three of us were guilty of forgetting who we were to each other. Priorities were shifted and the stress of daily life took over. I love how God woke me up, reminded me that He and He alone created my sister. He is well-aware of her strengths and her weaknesses. He knew exactly how He would use her during my mom's health crises, and He knew that in doing so, He would rekindle the spark we all once shared. He orchestrated everything in His perfect timing so she could take a year off work and care for our mother. There were no financial worries and no stress from her very demanding job.

Here's the thing about Kim...she is her father's daughter in all the great ways. She is funny. She loves to be social. She is the most hospitable person I know. She will bend over backwards to help you. She has no filter, which often has family members in gales of laughter and perhaps a little embarrassment also. There are many T.M.I. moments with Kim. There is no facade with her, what you see is what you get—period! Kim and I are different. She is extroverted, I am introverted. She lives in the city. I live in the country. My boys are like oil and water compared to her two kids. We also married two different men with two very different occupations, but the beauty is we all love each other. It's not perfect, but this is where the *what you see is what you get* comes in. No one ever wonders what a family get-together is going to be like. Our get-togethers are a cluster. They are filled with laughter, lots of talking (sometimes over one another), and maybe a little eye rolling, but it's who we are. I have a lot of memories of Kim, but one of my most vivid memories was in the fall of 1991. I was 17. Kim was 13. She had just discovered my dad was having an affair and our parent's marriage was dissolving before our very eyes. I was in my senior year of high school and had been out with friends. When I walked in the door that night, Kim was waiting for me. With tears in her eyes, she wrapped her arms around me and cried, wanting me to reassure her that Mom and Dad would be okay. I couldn't reassure her. I knew their marriage was failing. At that moment I knew no one this side of heaven would understand my history better than my sister.

Kim and I are four years apart. My boys are also four years apart. They argue like nobody's business, but I constantly remind them that one day I hope they realize no one will understand their history or where they came from better than each other. Kim was there to shave my legs when I was on complete bed rest with my oldest son, Jay. She was there to take care of my youngest son, Nick, when I had to have gallbladder surgery six weeks after giving birth to him (because although my husband is a wonderful father, he stunk with babies). In 2016, I experienced some health issues, and one day I unexpectedly needed a ride to the doctor. Kim was getting highlights in her hair. She demanded the highlights be rinsed out and she came to my rescue, wet head and all. When Kim and I were taking care of Mom, we shared many laughs and no one truly understood the joys and frustrations better than Kim.

Chapter 12

John & Walker ~ The Men in Mom's Life

There is nothing truer in this world than the love of a good dog.
~Mira Grant

Amy

When Mom started intense physical therapy after her first stroke, we knew her arm would need the most work. My dear friend Mary had mentioned that perhaps her husband John (a personal trainer, chef, and physical therapy aide… yes, he's all that!) could come to Mom's house and work with her as a way to give her some extra therapy on her arm and provide some much-needed encouragement. Mom readily agreed. John was and continues to be a huge blessing to Mom. He's relentless with his encouragement. Every time I asked Mom how her session with John was, she would reply, "I just love him." It helps that John is easy on the eyes, and he required her to put her bad arm around him after every session for a hug. When physical therapy ended, John continued to make weekly house calls to provide arm therapy. Eventually, John started cooking for Mom, which helped tremendously with her diabetes. I joke with John often that when the time comes for him to stand in front of God, and God asks him what he did with the talents He gave him, John can confidently and happily reply that he served Susan Brumme!

Kim

Mom and I went to rehabilitation therapy twice a week. She had a delightful occupational therapist, and while working on Mom's arm, we chatted a lot. The therapist knew that Mom was working with John at home, and he came up a lot in conversation. One day, the therapist was doing an arm movement with Mom when she remarked that she did that exact movement with John. Then in her sweet voice she boldly added, "And we kiss." I of course reacted with surprise. I figured a peck on the cheek was a great way to motivate her to get that arm moving! That John, he was always thinking!

During Mom's recovery, I was with her daily and would occasionally suggest things such as drinking more water, wearing a leg brace, or doing certain exercises. I even made her charts. Later, I asked her how much water she drank. It was never enough. I'd inquire if she did her exercises. She didn't. I'd ask, "Are you going to wear that brace?" She'd reply, "No, not today." Then John would come over to tell her to drink more water and she would tell me she drank more water because John told her to. I'd come over and she'd have her ankle brace on. I'd say, "Oh good, you have your brace on." Mom would reply, "John told me I should be wearing it all the time to support my ankle." Nothing seemed to stick unless John told her. One time, Amy and I thought she might be taking too much medication for her hurt ankle. Mom just pooh-poohed us. We called John, who told her how much she should be taking. For him, she readily complied. So basically, when we need Mom to do something, we just have John address it. God bless you, John!

Amy

After Mom's second stroke, she expressed an interest in getting a dog. Mom had not had a dog since we were kids. After her divorce, she was busy teaching and raising kids, and after retirement she traveled. But having two strokes changed things for her. When she first mentioned the dog thing to Kim and me, we looked at her like she was crazy. Selfishly, Kim and I didn't want the added responsibility of a dog; Mom was enough. However, we had a motto, "Whatever Mom wanted, Mom got," but this was really testing our rule. Mom would continue to mention getting a dog, and Kim and I would smile, nod our heads, and move on without addressing the request. When Mom was out of ear-shot, we would say things like, "What the heck is she thinking? Mom is not getting a dog," and toast our cocktail glasses in complete agreement. But then 2019 came along, a new year, a new beginning, and Mom was so much better. She needed Kim less and less, and could do more and more for herself. Suddenly, the dog idea didn't seem so crazy. As the winter wore on (and where we live, winters can be long and brutal), we realized a dog could be a real comfort for Mom. We started to talk about a fence and what kind of dog she wanted. Mom fell in love with my dog Cole years ago. Cole is a Vizsla. His personality is like a dopey college frat boy (think *Revenge of the Nerds*). Cole's dopiness doesn't mean he's not smart, just the opposite. Actually Vizslas are known for their intelligence, and he's wicked smart. Mom knew she didn't want to house train a dog, and she didn't want to mess with grooming a dog. She desperately wanted a dog just like Cole, a dog that would follow her around and cuddle with her. I contacted my breeder knowing that sometimes dogs come back to her when they are in a situation that hasn't worked out. Lo and behold, several months later my breeder had a two-year-old Vizsla who had been displaced. He had lived with two other families—so he was technically a rescue dog—and wouldn't you know it, he was also Cole's brother (but not from the same litter). When Mom met Walker, she knew he was her dog. Walker immediately honed in on Mom's "bad" arm, knowing she couldn't move it, and proceeded to lick her hand like crazy. Walker was a blessing to Mom, and Mom was a blessing to Walker. It brought so much joy to Kim and me knowing how happy they made each other. As time wore on, Mom and Walker did just about everything together. He became her sidekick. When Mom came to visit, so did Walker. When Mom had errands to run in town, Walker joined her, and on occasion, Mom would take Walker out for ice cream. My oldest son, Jay, affectionately referred to Walker as "Nana's high school boyfriend." Often, when I called Mom in the morning, she was reading her devotions with her dog right next to her. Yes, Mom had become one of those "dog moms." He's provided her with laughter, companionship, and love. Mom and I chuckle, because for years she wondered why God didn't put a man in her life in retirement. God actually did put a man in her life, we just had no idea it would be a furry, four-legged one named Walker!

Kim

I spent every day with Mom after her second stroke. I was the one who answered all of Mom's needs, so a dog…no way! Mom wasn't stable enough. A dog would knock her over. I'd be the one who had to clean up after it, and if something happened to her, I would become a dog owner. Every time Mom brought it up, I humored her, but secretly I completely opposed the idea. As spring approached and Mom kept improving, Amy and I finally decided we could give the dog thing a try. It would make Mom really happy. Amy did all the legwork to find Walker. I helped get a crate and get her home dog-ready. Amy got a fence installed and made vet appointments. Amy and her husband Mike committed to watching the dog when Mom took a trip or as necessary. So, Mom got her dog.

This special, and I do mean special, dog has been a true blessing. He keeps us on our toes, in a good way, and Mom just loves him so much.

Now when I see Mom, I ask her, "What did Walker do today?" She always has a story. Apparently, he loves eating birds and takes great delight in chasing them on her deck.

One day, I got to Mom's and she was standing by her sliding glass door trying to tell me what he did. Sometimes Mom's speech can be pretty broken. She was waving her arm up and down and said, "Bird!" She then made a splat movement and said, "Dead!" She then finished with, "Walker." I filled in the blanks. I said, "Mom, a bird flew into the window and died, and Walker finished it off!" Yep! I asked Mom what she did with the bird. She showed me a newspaper and said, "Recycle bin." I told Mom that birds were not recyclable and that nasty rotting dead bird would stay in her recycle bin for a week. She then held up two fingers, which meant recycling didn't get picked up for two more weeks! We had a good laugh, and I disposed of the bird properly. Another day, Mom asked me to replace the "springy thing" that holds the toilet paper roll because it fell off and Walker ate it! Walker also loved to destroy beds Mom had made. When I asked her why she didn't just close the bedroom doors after she made the beds, she said, "Oh, I don't mind, he likes it." Whatever Walker likes, Walker gets, and Mom is amused by him each and every day.

Chapter 13

Sanibel

(January 2019)

I remain confident of this:
I will see the goodness of the LORD in the land of the living.
Wait for the LORD; be strong and take heart and wait for the LORD.

~Psalm 27:13-14

Amy

In late 2018, Mom proposed the three of us take a trip to Sanibel Island, Florida. We thought it was a great way to say goodbye to 2018, and celebrate new beginnings in 2019. Kim and I readily agreed. Days before the trip, I called Kim to go over anything Mom might need or anything Kim needed me to do before we left. As I went through my list of questions, Kim cut me off before I even finished most of my task list, because she had already taken care of and thought of everything, as usual. Yes, she had checked with TSA about Mom getting through security with her sensor. Yes, she had purchased a pillbox that would house her pills for two weeks just in case we got stuck in Florida longer than anticipated. Yes, she had gotten Mom a case she could take with her to hold her diabetic supplies on the plane. Yes, she was going over to help Mom pack. Kim even took pictures of the personal hygiene items she was going to pack for Mom, so that I didn't pack the same items for myself. The only thing that ever occurred to me for the trip planning was requesting a wheelchair for Mom (if she needed it) at the airport. If preparing Mom for the trip was left up to me,

I'm pretty sure I'd be in tears at some point because I didn't plan accordingly. Trust me, pills would have been unaccounted for, and knowing me, I would have forgotten her insulin! After all, I was the girl who went to Disney on an anniversary trip with her husband in wedge sandals because they were "cute." One day into the trip, my feet were on fire. I ended up paying way too much for a cheap pair of sneakers with Mickey Mouse on them to get me through the remainder of the trip. Thinking of everything and being prepared and organized is just one of my sister's many strengths, from handling all of Mom's prescriptions to figuring out her pump. If it weren't for my sister's sacrifice of her time and finances, the stress of juggling everything for Mom would have consumed and stressed us all out, and wouldn't have had the outcome God intended for the three of us. Mostly, Kim was kind and patient, and isn't that what really matters? When I think of myself in my old age, I pray for a caregiver like my sister: a person who is all heart, who is not only organized and smart, but cares, really cares, and demonstrates it through daily kindness.

Kim

Let's not forget while I was taking care of Mom, Amy was taking care of me. She always knew what to say and how to help whenever I needed anything. We all deserved that wonderful trip to Sanibel. Sanibel is a pretty island. Amy and I got up every morning for a walk, then the three of us relaxed on the porch with our coffee. We basked in the sun all afternoon, usually with cocktails. We had wonderful food and conversation. We also did some great shopping. One afternoon, Mom really wanted to go to a trendy Florida store that her friend Donna had once taken her to. It was in Fort Myers, a forty-five-minute drive away. Amy and I had no desire to go, but we worked off our motto, "Whatever Mom wants, Mom gets," and we agreed to take her. We piled into the car and headed to Fort Meyers. We pulled into the shopping center and went inside. Mom immediately went to the bathroom (as usual), then she poked around. Only a few minutes later, she announced, "I don't like any of this stuff. Let's leave." Amy and I looked at each other and rolled our eyes. We could have been mad, but we shrugged it off and laughed when Mom added, "I don't think that was the store Donna took me to." Amy and I were thrilled to be returning to our condo so soon. The Sanibel trip was exactly what we needed. Our parents, who deeply loved each other, divorced after twenty years of marriage. Dad survived twenty-two years more with a brain tumor and debilitating stroke, then died a quick but horrific death. Four months after his death, we watched our mother lay in a hospital bed unable to move or speak after suffering a massive stroke. We feared her death, or her having to live a life just like my father had. Thankfully, she did recover, not completely, but as we like to say "good enough." As I gazed up at the sun in the middle of January on a beautiful island, I felt filled with complete joy. Why? God is good, and blesses us even in our hardest times!

Amy

Mom, Kim, and I drove across a long bridge, admiring the ocean on each side, cruising towards Sanibel Island, Florida. The clear water glistened from the sun's bright rays. The sunroof on our rental car stood open, and a cool breeze circulated. On the radio, Mom's favorite tunes blasted from the oldies station. I was driving and Kim was in the front seat navigating our way to our island oasis for the week. Mom relaxed in the back seat, looking out the window smiling. We reminisced about the last time we were in Sanibel. Kim was eleven, and I was fifteen. At the time, we were a perfect family enjoying a wonderful summer vacation. Mom and Dad were happily married, we were healthy, and all was well with the world.

Back then we could have never predicted what would happen to our family. Now, as we crossed over that long bridge to our vacation destination, we took in deep breaths, feeling bonded together by all we'd endured and by the love we have for one another. We breathed out, confident our faith has helped us survive. We smiled because we are truly blessed. We reflected on the past year with thankful hearts, knowing that what binds us together makes us stronger. Our bond can never be broken. As Kim and I looked at Mom in the back seat, smiling, she sweetly said, "I'm just so happy."

Epilogue

One Year Post Stroke
(July 1, 2019)

Amy

As a Christian, I try not to question God's timing, and to be honest, much of God's timing during my life has made sense to me. As Mom's one-year stroke anniversary approached, however, His timing made no sense to me. Kim and I had planned a huge "one-year stroke party" for Mom to celebrate her success. We were so excited, and so was Mom. Then on July 1, Mom was walking up concrete steps with Kim and her kids (headed to watch Luke and Lauren's swim lessons) when she tripped and fell on her "bad leg." She did not break anything, but we learned that honestly, she might have been better off if she did. Instead, she strained ligaments. By July 6, I took Walker home with me because she could no longer care for him. By July 10, Kim and I had to put Mom in a short-term rehab facility because she could no longer care for herself. We canceled her one-year stroke party and never rescheduled. Mom also missed her fiftieth class reunion, which she was so looking forward to. I couldn't believe Mom—and yes, Kim and I too—were spending another July in a rehab facility. I thought God must be joking! Surely, He didn't mean for that to happen, but it did, and it rocked Mom, Kim, and me to our core. After spending three weeks in rehab, she returned home, and continues to make progress. She and Walker were thrilled to be reunited.

During Mom's first year of recovery, we faced many struggles but there were just as many blessings. It is true that sometimes the blessings were hard to see, especially when she was in yet another rehab facility, but as I look back during that time I see all the good that came from it. The people who helped us along the way were limitless in their determination. My relationship with my sister was cemented, and our mother, although her life looks different, did recover. God organized the people and events perfectly, as He promises us. Through the good, the bad, and the ugly, He never left us. Through our struggles and suffering, He blessed us.

Mom and Dad's engagement picture

Amy and Kim ages four and eight

Dad's bug costume for Halloween. Amy age 13, Kim age 9

Dad remodeling our house

Family Picture 1989

Mom, Kim, and Amy in matching outfits. Amy age 17, Kim age 13

Kim, Mom, and Amy 1996

Lauren and Luke with Grandpa Brad at the nursing home

Kim and Dad in the car on his last car ride

Mom and her grandkids. Jay age 12, Nick age 8, Lauren age 7, Luke age 3

Amy and Kim with Aunt Karen

Mom's 67 birthday party, just 2 days before Dad got sick

Fall 2018, Amy's family, Kim's family and Mom all in our Team Sue shirts

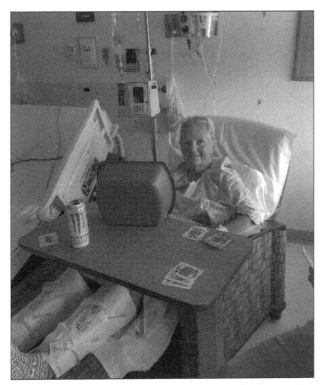

Mom playing cards in the hospital a week after her stroke

Amy and Kim in Sanibel

Mom and Amy in Sanibel

About the Authors

Romans 8:28
God works for the
good of those who
love him

Amy and Kim grew up in Central Illinois. Amy Siebert now lives in Danvers, Illinois, with her husband and two sons. She works for an insurance company and attends Eastview Christian Church in Bloomington. Kim Stille lives in Bloomington, Illinois, with her husband and two children. She is a 3rd-grade teacher and attends College Park Christian Church.

Amy and Kim both graduated from Illinois State University. *Dear Mom and Dad: A Love Letter to Our Parents* is their first book. Amy has blogged for years (www.siebertfamily4.blog-spot.com) and has always wanted to write a book. Kim has not! When tragedy struck their family and tested their faith, they decided what better way to share their story than to write a book. From childhood to adulthood they persevere the only way they know how—by relying on God, leaning on each other, and even laughing along the way.

Made in the USA
Columbia, SC
19 September 2020